I0560775

# A JUMP FROM EVIL ALTAR

RESIST ATTACKS, REJECT EVIL
ARROWS FROM EVIL ALTARS

## PRAYER M. MADUEKE

ISBN: 978-1964584102

Published by Prayer Publications.

Printed in the United States of America.

# 4 Free Ebooks

In order to say a 'Thank You' for purchasing *A Jump from Evil Altar*, I offer these books to you in appreciation. Click or type **madueke.com/free-gift** in your browser.

# Message from the Author

I want to see you succeed, grow, and break free from negativity and obstacles. My hope is for you to thrive, unaffected by negative influences and challenging situations. Because of that, please permit me to introduce two courses that I believe passionately will help you:

1. To break the evil altars and powers of your father's house, The role of altars in the realm of existence is very key because altars are meeting places between the physical and the spiritual, between the visible and the invisible.

   Unless a man cuts off the evil flow from the power of his father's house, he will not fulfil his destiny. Click here to learn more about my course on how to tear down unholy altars and close the enemy's entryways into your life!

2. To help you seamlessly break iron-like problems, illness, delayed marriage, poverty, or any long-standing battle.

   Discover the transformative power of Christian fasting and prayer. Remember, Matthew 17:21 teaches us, *"But this kind of demon does not go out except by prayer and fasting."* Ready to overcome your struggles? <u>Click here</u> to learn more about this course.

Embrace the journey ahead with faith, for through prayer, fasting, and the dismantling of evil altars, you shall unlock the doors to spiritual liberation and divine breakthrough. May your path be illuminated by His grace as you walk towards a life free from bondage.

If you're seeing this from the physical copy, type the link: <u>madueke.com/courses</u> in your browser to view all the courses on my website.

**Prayer Madueke**
CHRISTIAN AUTHOR

# Christian Counselling

We were created for a greater purpose than only survival and God wants us to live a full life.

If you need prayer or counselling, or if you have any other inquiries, please visit the counselling page on my website to know when I will be available for a phone call.

Click or type **links.madueke.com/counselling** in your browser.

# Let's Connect on Youtube ▶

Join me on my YouTube channel, "Prayer M. Madueke," where I share powerful insights, guidance, and prayers for spiritual breakthroughs.

Subscribe today to unlock the secrets of the Kingdom and embrace an abundant life. Let's grow together!

Click or type links.madueke.com/youtube in your browser.

# TABLE OF CONTENTS

# ACKNOWLEDGMENTS

The writing of a book necessarily involves many people. Therefore, my first gratitude goes to Almighty God, who gave me the strength and wisdom to put down my thoughts and inspiration on paper. Glory be to our Lord and Savior, Jesus Christ.

Foremost among those to whom I owe a debt of gratitude is Dr D. K. Olukoya, General overseer of the Mountain of Fire and Miracles Ministries. He happily read the manuscript and approved it for publication.

Finally, my gratitude goes to my wife, Roseline C. Madueke, and my children, who had to bear the brunt of the many hours I denied them that love that is so essential in a happy relationship.

# CHAPTER 1

# INTRODUCTION

The children of Israel sinned against God, and God delivered them into the hands of their enemies. Thus, the Israelites became their servants. In addition, because of these Midianites, the children of Israel made themselves the dens, which are in the mountains and caves and strongholds. The Israelites saw that the Midianites, Amalekites, and even the children of the East came up against them, with their cattle in their tents. They came in a multitude like grasshoppers on their camels and destroyed all their increase of the earth, leaving neither sheep, oxen nor asses for them. The children of Israel then became impoverished because of their enemies.

As the Israelites were in terrible afflictions of distress, instead of repenting, they started looking for solutions in a wrong way, by building alters, just like the heathen nations around them. Each family began to build altars. However, their condition got worse even with the altars. After seven years, they cried unto the Lord. Let us see Judges 6:1, 6.

> *"And the children of Israel did evil in the sight of the LORD: and the LORD delivered them into the hand of Midian seven years... And Israel was greatly impoverished because of the Midianites; and the children of Israel cried unto the LORD"* (Judges 6:1, 6).

When they cried to God, He sent a prophet to them who reminded them of the goodness of God. Yet they despised the Lord by fearing the gods of the Amorites, for who they built altars (see the Book of Judges, 6:11-12)

*"And there came an angel of the LORD, and sat under an oak which was in Ophrah, that pertained unto Joash the Abi–ezrite: and his son Gideon threshed wheat by the winepress, to hide it from the Midianites. And the angel of the LORD appeared unto him, and said unto him, The LORD is with thee, thou mighty man of valour"* (Judges, 6:11-12).

The Lord is with many believers today but they do not know. Many mighty people of God today are still serving under great bondage. There are much great potential deposited in many believers today but these believers are still living in sin.

One can have all that it takes to succeed and still fail in life. You can be a mighty man of valour and still fail in life (see the book of Judges 6:13).

Believers should try to find out just like Gideon did through prayers, why they pass through difficulties despite the fact that they are born again. The clear point is that miracles will not come our way until the evil altars militating against our spiritual and physical welfare are destroyed. We need to destroy the evil altars and build an altar unto the Lord our God upon the Rock of Ages (Judges 6:25-27).

An altar can be built to destroy an individual, a family, a group or even a whole nation. Korah, the son of Izhar, the son of Koliath, the son of Levi; Dathan and Abiram, the sons of Eliab; and On, the son of Peleth; the sons of Reuben, were under a curse.

> *"Reuben, thou art my firstborn, my might, and the beginning of my strength, the excellency of dignity, and the excellency of power: Unstable as water, thou shalt not excel; because thou wentest up to thy father's bed; then defiledst thou it: he went up to my couch" (Genesis 49: 3-4).*

The people who were more than two hundred and fifty princes of the assembly; famous in the congregation; men of renown, gathered themselves together against Moses and Aaron. Every attempt to call them to order failed and Moses challenged their own prayers on the evil altar standing on the holy altar of God.

> *"And Moses was very wroth, and said unto the LORD, Respect not thou their offering: I have*

*not taken one ass from them, neither have I hurt*
*one of them" (Numbers 16:15).*

When a determined enemy has vowed, and entered into a covenant with evil spirits to kill, if repentance is despised, there must be death. If the righteous person refuses to pray, he may die.

*"And there came out a fire from the LORD, and*
*consumed the two hundred and fifty men that*
*offered incense... "Now they that died in the*
*plague were fourteen thousand and seven*
*hundred, beside them that died about the matter*
*of Korah" (Numbers 16:35, 49).*

This was an attack against Moses and Aaron, the leaders of Israel. Many true believers are dying today because they refuse to pray the right prayers. Abel died through household wickedness because he refused to pray the right prayers. Many are rendered useless, poor, sick and turned to perpetual servants because they refused to fight evil altars and their evil priests.

There was an altar built by King Jeroboam in Israel, which enslaved many lives there. By the powers of that altar, many people's destinies were caged and amputated. The evil priest, King Jeroboam, ruled the people unchallenged until one day. There came a man of God out of Judah by the word of God. That was the first time the altar and its priest was challenged and put to shame (1 Kings 13:15). Many Christians have not prayed and given challenge to their family evil altars; and that is the reason why they are living below their divine standard. God is waiting for you to take the lead. Many evil priests cannot repent unless they are challenged. Some altars are raised against a whole nation

*"And Balaam said unto Balak, Build me here seven altars, and prepare me here seven oxen and seven rams. ²And Balak did as Balaam had spoken; and Balak and Balaam offered on every altar a bullock and a ram" (Numbers 23: 1-2).*

Balaam and Balak built altars against the children of Israel when they came out from Egypt. The number 'seven,' means perfection or completeness in biblical/prophetic interpretation. The seven evil altars were erected against Israel to make sure that none of them escaped alive.

*"And he returned unto him, and, lo, he stood by his burnt sacrifice, he, and all the princes of Moab... For from the top of the rocks I see him, and from the hills I behold him: lo, the people*

*shall dwell alone, and shall not be reckoned
among the nations" (Numbers 23:6, 9).*

When they summoned the nation of Israel, the people
appeared from the top of the rocks. Balaam saw them but
could not harm them. The lives of the children of Israel
were too hot for him. Instead of destruction, Balaam saw
the blessing of God for Israel. Balak was a wicked king,
who was determined to finish a whole nation on an evil
altar. He failed the first time but asked Balaam to go with
him to another place provided the children of Israel were
cursed, even if it required cursing only a few of them. His
aim was to curse and destroy all of them but when he
failed in the first attempt, he then decided to curse some
of them.

*"And Balak said unto him, Come, I pray thee,
with me unto another place, from whence thou
mayest see them: thou shalt see but the utmost
part of them, and shalt not see them all: and
curse me them from thence" (Numbers 23:13).*

When an individual is called on the evil altar for
destruction and the evil priest fails to destroy him or her,
they (satanic agents) may decide to summon the person's
womb (if it is a woman), in order to bring the curse of

barrenness on her. Alternatively, they can summon one's eyes, legs, business, certificates, marriages etc. It is very unfortunate to say that many believers' marriages are on evil altars.

Balak and Balaam went to the evil field of Zophim; to the top of Pisgah, and built seven evil altars. The field of Zophim was a place of sacrifice where evil priests consulted demons to destroy human beings, property, and to cage people's destines.

In Zophim, there was an elevated top called the top of Pisgah, where the highest demons were summoned. There, they could locate anybody, place, or thing easily. There, Balak and Balaam built seven altars, offered bullock, and a ram on every altar. When a holy man of God joins an evil person to pray against a child of God, his prayers will become witchcraft; sacrifice on an evil altar. Many churches today are praying against true Christians and churches; thereby, turning their congregations to evil altars. Many well-gifted ministers have allowed the love of money to destroy their ministries, by receiving money from sinners in order to pray against their fellow human beings who are living right with God.

*"But godliness with contentment is great gain. For we brought nothing into this world and it is certain we can carry no thing out. And having food and raiment let us be therewith content. But they that will be rich fall into temptation and a snare, and into many foolish and hurtful lusts, which drown men in destruction and perdition. For the love of money is the root of all evil: which while some coveted after, they have erred from the faith, and pierced themselves through with many sorrows"* (1 Timothy 6:6-10).

Evil communications corrupts good manners. Nobody can bribe God. You can bribe your pastor to take sides with you to destroy another person but you cannot bribe God. Whenever a man stands with God, prays the right prayers and lives a perfect life of holiness, no power will destroy him or her. The Bible says that the Lord met Balaam and put words in his mouth, and said, go again unto Balak.

The Lord will send your Balaam back to your Balak. That is what we call "back to sender." What every agent of Satan is afraid of is what God has said about your life. One thing they want to know about a person is what God has said concerning him or her. Once they know the will of God concerning your life, they will fight to take you away from that position. They will make sure that you do not even know what God says about you. In addition, unfortunately, only few people know the will of God for their lives.

> *"And he said unto Balak, Stand here by thy burnt offering, while I meet the LORD yonder. And the LORD met Balaam, and put a word in his mouth, and said, Go again unto Balak, and say thus. And when he came to him, behold, he stood by his burnt offering, and the princes of Moab with him. And Balak said unto him, what hath the LORD spoken?" (Numbers 23:15-17).*

Many enemies, "kings" and "princes" are standing on evil altars by their burnt offerings asking your Balaam what God has said about you. Yet many are not even concerned to know what God is saying at this hour (verse 17). Once your enemies know what God has spoken concerning your life, marriage, business, academics, work, and in fact, your whole future, they will begin to fight. Some people's files containing what God has said about them are on evil altars and need to be withdrawn.

When Satan knows what God has said about you and you do not know, it is a problem. When your enemies know what God has said about you and you do not know it, is a very serious problem. When you know what God has said about you but you are not to working towards the manifestation, it becomes even worse for you. When God says something good about you but you are a sinner, it becomes a more serious problem. If you are a Christian but what God has said about you is not manifesting, it is also a problem.

## WHAT GOD SAID CONCERNING ISRAEL

*"And when he came to him, behold, he stood by his burnt offering, and the princes of Moab with him. And Balak said unto him, what hath the LORD spoken? And he took up his parable, and said, Rise up, Balak, and hear; hearken unto me, thou son of Zippor: God is not a man, that he should lie; neither the son of man, that he should repent: hath he said, and shall he not do it? Or hath he spoken, and shall he not make it good? Behold, I have received commandment to bless: and he hath blessed; and I cannot reverse it. Behold, the people shall rise up as a great*

*lion, and lift up himself as a young lion: he shall*
*not lie down until he eat of the prey, and drink*
*the blood of the slain" (Numbers 23:17-20, 24).*

1.  Israel shall rise up as a great lion and lift himself up as a young lion.

2.  He shall not lie down until he eats up the prey, and drinks the blood of the slain.

3.  He shall pour the water out of his buckets (Numbers 24:7).

4.  His seed shall be in many waters (Numbers 24:7).

5.  His king shall be higher than Agag (Numbers 24:7).

6.  His kingdom shall be exalted (Numbers 24:7).

7.  He shall eat up the enemy nations and shall break their bones and pierce them through with his arrows (Numbers 24:8, 17-25).

With these wonderful promises, Israel still failed and the people were destroyed on the evil altars (Numbers 23:27-30). Balak and Balaam went to the highest evil altars of their time and deposited Israel and everything concerning the nation on evil altars. The highest evil altar at that time was at the topmost hill of Peor, "that looketh toward Jeshimon." The top of Peor was the habitation of every kind of demon. In addition, evil altar built there could locate a person in any nation of the world in a moment and it had the ability to retain names, blessings and other things. Once summoned there, even if you were not harmed at that moment, your name could be retained there and a monitoring demon released to report you for evil action as you commit sin.

Verse 28 says: "And Balak brought Balaam unto the top of Peor that looked toward Jeshimon." Jeshimon was the evil bush where Baal worshippers usually went to worship Baal.

Little children and pregnant women were offered as items of sacrifice to demons at the evil altars in the bush of Jeshimon. This was where Balak and Balaam took to the children of Israel spiritually with the princes of Moab. Though the Israelites could not be harmed at that time, they were spiritually deposited there and monitoring demons, (spirits) were released to make them commit sin. These were the demons that should report them to the satanic kingdom in their weak moments. These demons were also to report them for evil action as soon as they departed from righteousness and committed any kind of sin. These were also the spirits that should monitor them and bring "perverseness" in Israel, the spirits that opposed righteousness. These spirits fertilized enchantments and divinations. In addition, unfortunately for the children of Israel, they were ignorant of what Balak, the Princes of Moab, and Balaam had done against them on the evil altars.

Some people who know that evil men are calling them on evil altars do not know how to withdraw their names, blessings, marriages, etc., from evil altars. Some do not believe in deliverance, so they do not mind whatever any man or woman says about them on the evil altars. Yet some people were dedicated and deposited before they were even born. Some were deposited there by "concerned" parents, occult relations, and enemies. Some voluntarily dedicated themselves ignorantly. The enemies of Israel dedicated them on the evil altars.

> *"And Balaam said unto Balak, Build me here seven altars, and prepare me here seven oxen and seven rams. And Balak did as Balaam had spoken; and Balak and Balaam offered on every altar a bullock and a ram.... And he brought him into the field of Zophim, to the top of Pisgah, and built seven altars, and offered a bullock and a*

*ram on every altar…And Balak said unto Balaam, Come, I pray thee, I will bring thee unto another place; peradventure it will please God that thou mayest curse me them from thence. And Balak brought Balaam unto the top of Peor that looketh toward Jeshimon. And Balaam said unto Balak, Build me here seven altars, and prepare me here seven bullocks and seven rams. And Balak did as Balaam had said, and offered a bullock and a ram on every altar" (Numbers 23:1-2, 14, 27-30).*

Many good Christians who preach and believe in holiness and live pure lives; who are baptized and filled with the Holy Ghost but do not believe in deliverance and as a result, do not pray the right prayers, are being constantly attacked by monitoring demons from evil altars; who have been assigned to separate them from righteousness and their God.

Many good Christians are suffering many setbacks in their Christian lives, businesses, marriages, academics, work, etc., because of attacks constantly coming from evil altars. Break the link and the spirits will flee!

*"Submit yourselves therefore to God. Resist the devil, and he will flee from you" (James 4:7).*

All those little evil thoughts, unbelief, ignorance, or moments of spiritual weakness can destroy much in the life of a good Christian who has not broken the evil links with evil altars. When a good minister or true child of God refuses to break all links with evil altars, he may need to fight more than Alexander the Great every day of his life without total victory in certain aspects of his life. This is because the evil bridge will continue to link demons to every department of his life. He may be holy but he will be fighting the same demon every day. He will be dying in instalments, as he will be suffering from health failure, business failure, and poverty. He may have a permanent reproach, shame and stubborn problem that will be mocking his God.

Such Christians may die not because it is the will of God for them but because of lack of knowledge. They may go to heaven like Lazarus the beggar, who was laid at the gate of one rich sinner, whose desire was to be fed with the crumbs that fell from the rich man's table. His body was full of sores, and dogs were eating his flesh while he was still alive. Thanks be to God that when, he died, he was carried by angels into Abraham's bosom. He made it at last. He came to the street of gold, the new heaven.

> *"And there was a certain beggar named Lazarus, which was laid at his gate, full of sores, and desiring to be fed with the crumbs which fell from the rich man's table: moreover the dogs came and licked his sores" (Luke 16:20- 21).*

He had the privilege of a new relationship with God the Father, God the Son, and God the Holy Spirit. He was among the possessors of new rewards. He arrived at the new Jerusalem; the great city; the eternal city; the holy city; the city unstained with sin; the eternal residence of the bride of Christ and all the saints of all ages. A city where everything is as clear as crystal. It is a city that has gates that shall not be shut at all. There shall be no night, no obstructions, and nothing to block the glory of God. The city has a good design and perfect symmetry.

> *"And, behold, I come quickly; and my reward is with me, to give every man according as his work shall be.... Blessed are they that do his commandments that they may have right to the tree of life, and may enter in through the gates into the city.... I Jesus have sent mine angel to*

*testify unto you these things in the churches. I am the root and the offspring of David, and the bright and morning star. And the Spirit and the bride say, Come. And let him that heareth say, Come. And let him that is athirst come. And whosoever will, let him take the water of life freely.... The grace of our Lord Jesus Christ be with you all. Amen" (Revelation 22:12, 14, 16-17, 21).*

This is the city where the tree of life is; the tree that yields different types of fruit each month. The leaves of the tree are for the healing of the nations.

*"In the midst of the street of it, and on either side of the river, was there the tree of life, which bare twelve manner of fruits, and yielded her fruit every month: and the leaves of the tree were for the healing of the nations" (Revelation 22:2).*

This was the city that angels took Lazarus to and Lazarus is still there and will forever be there. I want to go to heaven at all cost but not like Lazarus. By the grace of God, my going to heaven is necessary but my prayer is that it will not be like that of Lazarus a man that went to heaven without personal accommodation. He was taken direct to the bosom of Abraham.

The rich man wanted Lazarus in hell as a servant (<u>Luke 16:22-31</u>). Lazarus did not resist the rich man's request. In the same vein, many Christians are not resisting satanic requests for their lives these days. By the grace of God, I will go to heaven but not like Lazarus, I will go to heaven but not like Abel who allowed his brother, Cain, to terminate his life and destroy his destiny. I would like to go to heaven like Abraham, the man who possessed his possession here and there. I would like to go to heaven like Joshua and Caleb, men who served their God and possessed their possessions too.

Even if your foundation is like that of Rahab- a woman born into prostitution- or like that of Ruth of Moab (the nation that worshipped a wall as god and practiced witchcraft), you can change camp here. You can cross over and become a man or woman of God with eternal blessings waiting for you. God forbid that I go to heaven like Samson, a man mocked by the Philistines, as his two eyes were plucked out. He was a great man of God who died in the camp of sinners (though he made it to heaven).

Everyone attached to Naomi at Moab died but she survived and made it. Hannah, the mother of Samuel, must have also made it among the women of her days. Although David made many mistakes, he made it to heaven eventually. He is now in his mansion in heaven - in the company of angels. This is not where Saul, the first king of Israel is. By the grace of God, my going to heaven will be like that of Enoch and Elijah.

God forbid that I end up like Gehazi who inherited Naaman's leprosy! Naaman crossed over. So what are you waiting for? King Nebuchadnezzar might have killed the people of all nations but not Daniel, Shedrach, Meshack and Abednego. Herod might have killed John the Baptist. James may be beheaded but Paul and Silas prayed themselves out.

All the above people went to heaven but in different ways. How do you want to go to heaven? In the days of Jesus, many people died of hunger because they refused his food (Matthew 14:15-21). Those who were determined were delivered (see Matthew 4:23-25). He (Jesus) healed a man with withered hands (Matthew 12:10-13). A man with an unclean spirit was also delivered (Mark 1:23-29). He destroyed barrenness in the life of Elizabeth. In the Book of John, Jesus raised a dead young man who was being carried out of a city- the only son of his mother - between the city gate and the grave. In the Acts of the Apostles, through the name of Jesus, His disciples raised Dorcas. Do not die like Lazarus, even if you will make it to heaven.

Here is an example of a fulfilled destiny:

> *"For David, after he had served his own generation by the will of God, fell on sleep, and was laid unto his fathers, and saw corruption"* (Acts 13:36).

King David died but that was after he had served his own generation according to the will of God. Everybody is going to pass through death except those who will be alive in Christ on the day of the rapture (1 Thessalonians 4:16-17). We all know that death is certain. However, what we do with our lives now matters so much. Many have died without fulfilling their destiny. One outstanding man that fulfilled his destiny is David.

David, the son of Jesse was one of the most prominent Bible characters in Old Testament history. He was a shepherd. The enemy wanted to confine him to that lie but he moved ahead by prayer and righteousness to become the player, whose music soothed the troubled spirit of King Saul. David was Israel's sweet psalmist as well as the youthful warrior who slew Goliath, and thus became the hero of the people. He was the beloved King with a humble spirit and was always conscious of his lowly family background, birthplace, occupation and service even while in the King's court.

As a shepherd of his father's flock he moved ahead by desires, prayers, faith and righteousness into Saul's house as a servant to him and a beloved friend to Prince Jonathan. He was loyal and devoted. From his lowly position, he was made a king who first reigned at Hebron, and then at Jerusalem over all Israel. With a wonderful combination of personal bravery, boldness, skill, and courage, he led Israel to subdue her enemies. Such as the Philistines, Canaanites, Moabites, Ammonites, Edomites and Amalekites. From his lowly position, he rose to be a champion, a great soldier and man of war, who conquered the supposedly impregnable city of Jerusalem and made it his capital.

He was the first in Israel to kill an enemy giant. He neither embezzled money nor ruled Israel for personal gain. The secret of David's victories was that he regarded and fought Israel's enemies as God's enemies and dedicated his spoils of war to the Lord. He was a man after God's heart. His reign was free from Idolatry and he was loyal to God in his testimonies and worship. David was the greatest king of Israel with an unusual wisdom in administration. However, not every part of his life was right and pure.

It is to be remembered however that it was in the period of apparent prosperity and divine favor that King David, committed immorality, conspiracy and murder. Even after his deep repentance, he still reaped the full consequences of his actions. Four of his children died prematurely because of Uriah whom he killed. In addition, having plotted and killed Uriah in the warfront, the spirit of war never left his family.

Though David was forgiven and by prayer, deep repentance and discipline, he overcame those spirits, many of his children like Amon, Absalom, Adonijah, and Solomon never overcame. For instance, one of David's sons known as Absalom messed up David's concubines in the presence of all Israel through the counsel of Ahitophel. In fact, the major, reason why David wept when Absalom died was because he knew that Absalom was born to be great but the spirit David invited into his family overcame him (Absalom). What happened was that David prayed himself out of that evil he invited into his family, i.e. family curse.

David's life was a mixture of the good and the ugly. His life was filled with noble deeds and accomplishments; yet stained with great sins of terrible consequences. Every aspect of his life provides rich lessons for pilgrims along the heavenly path: His childhood victories, family life, fall, repentance, life of faith, submission, forgiving spirit and kindness. He never remained where he failed. No evil altar held him captive for too long. However, he is not our perfect example. He also sinned in numbering Israel and was punished as a result. It serves as a warning to us. Sin buys temporary pleasure at a price of God's favor, eternal peace, and happiness. However, his life is not our ideal. There are spotless lessons to learn from, the lives of Enoch, Samuel, Daniel, and Joseph. Above all, Jesus is our perfect example (Heb.12:2).

Remember that David fought his battle and won at last, even on the day of his death (Acts 13:36). He is now walking in the streets of gold. The New Jerusalem will be a cube; measuring twelve thousand furlongs, approximately. It is one thousand, five hundred miles in length, breath, and height. In linear measurement, we discover that this glorious eternal city is two million, two hundred and fifty thousand square miles in one layer of mansions. Street will rise up over streets, one thousand, five hundred miles (Revelation 21:16-17). Millions of interesting layers of avenues are there. The city will easily contain billions of people. It is big enough for all who find the narrow way (see John 14:2; Matthew 7:14). This is where David is now, and you can be there if you wholeheartedly desire it.

## IMMORALITY IN THE CAMP

*"He hath not beheld iniquity in Jacob, neither hath he seen perverseness in Israel: the LORD his God is with him, and the shout of a king is among them....Surely there is no enchantment against Jacob, neither is there any divination against Israel: according to this time it shall be said of Jacob and of Israel, What hath God wrought!" (Numbers 23:21, 23).*

Before Balak and Balaam separated, Balaam gave Balak evil counsel. The secret of Israel's victory against the evil altar was righteousness. Balak sent beautiful daughters of Moab into the camp of the Israelites. The daughters of Moab were to dress half-nude to appear seductive. They were to put on transparent and perforated dresses; miniskirts, short gowns, topless and backs slacks. In fact, they had to dress in such a way that men would be enticed and therefore begin to lust after them. They were to dress that way and pass across the children of Israel in Shatter.

Balaam counselled Balak to find a way of using iniquity to remove righteousness from the camp of Israel, thereby, perverting the camp. He was sure once God sees iniquity in the camp, He (God would withdraw his support, protection and favor from the children of Israel); and the monitoring demons from the evil altars in the field of Zophim, at the top of Pisgah, and the one at the top of Peor that looks towards Jeshimon, would ring a bell and Israel would be attacked instantly.

Every strong evil altar retains information stored there and it can be there for thousands of years if it is not withdrawn. What your ancestors said to shrines concerning you before you were even born is still in satanic computers. All the promises your ancestors made to your family shrines and altars are very much fresh in the memory of your family's evil spirits until you fight with a better blood. An occult man can invoke demons from your family altars to pursue your life; and can renew the sickness, disease and evil that had ever operated in the lineages of your parents. A high occult personality can mandate a spirit to conduct a research in order to dig out the file containing every evil that has ever happened in your family linage. The details of your file from your mother's womb can be repeated in a moment of time on the evil altar. They know where your placenta was buried.

There was an intelligent woman undergraduate who was suddenly attacked by an incurable sickness. The problem continued to challenge from one form to another until she started having mental problems. She knew that she was getting mad but she did not know what to do. Over the years, she went to many hospitals and visited herbalists or native doctors, all to no avail. One of her concerned lecturers took her to a place where she saw in a mirror how she was born, her childhood life, the people she has ever met in life, how and when her problems started etc. She saw everything but the mirror did not tell her the way out. She saw the source of her problems but there was no solution. Under that confusion, she stumbled to our church. In my office, she underwent our deliverance ministration the following week, and that was the end of those problems. After about one year, the lecturer that took her to that evil mirror died mysteriously.

Sexual immorality, adultery and fornication are the most common forms of backsliding.

*"And Israel abode in Shittim, and the people*
*began to commit whoredom with the daughters of*
*Moab. And they called the people unto the*
*sacrifices of their gods: and the people did eat,*
*and bowed down to their gods. And Israel joined*
*himself unto Baal–peor: and the anger of the*
*LORD was kindled against Israel"* (Numbers
25:1-3).

These sins are usually entered into through carelessness
with the opposite sex. Samson, like other, Israelites, won
many battles. However, the spirit of immorality defeated
him. It has to be noted that immediately the children of
Israel went into sin of sexual immorality, they were
spiritually separated from God Almighty. The mercy and
love of God as well as other benefits were withdrawn
instantly. The records of their past lives were forgotten as
their names were blotted out of the Book of Life. They
were exposed to satanic oppression. The divine hedge of
security was broken, therefore they lacked direction. The
anger of God was kindled against them. There was real
confusion everywhere. And as they were weeping before
the door of the tabernacle of the congregation, one of the
children of Israel from the cursed tribe of Simeon
(Numbers 25:14) was marching with a Midianites woman

to bed (Numbers 25:6-7). Before Phinehas' intervention, twenty four thousand people had died in the plague. Our God is a God of judgment and mercy. Every believer should learn how to withdraw what our ancestors and our enemies have deposited on evil altars against us.

## DIVINE JUDGMENT AGAINST THE MIDIANITES

*"And the LORD spake unto Moses, saying, $^{17}$Vex the Midianites, and smite them" (Numbers 25:16-17).*

The wicked never goes unpunished. After the Lord had finished judging his people, the Israelites, He also judged the Midianites. In the judgment, all the five kings of Midian were killed. They were Evi, Rekem, Zur, Hur and Reba. Balaam was also killed with a sword (see Numbers 31:1-2). All the males and all the females that had known men by lying with him were killed also (Numbers 31:9, 15-17).

Evil altars are raised by the enemy to steal and destroy. Any sacrifice on an evil altar is food given to wicked spirits to seek their assistance in an evil altar. What then is an evil altar?

# PRAYER POINTS

1.  Any evil dedication against my life in any evil altar; break and release me, in the name of Jesus.

2.  Wherever I am being called on any evil altar; blood of Jesus, answer for me, in the name of Jesus.

3.  Every determined evil priest that has taken an oath to destroy me on the evil altar; fail woefully by fire, in the name of Jesus.

4.  I withdraw the totality of my life from the bondage in any evil altar, in the name of Jesus.

5.  Anything representing me on any evil altar; catch fire, in the name of Jesus.

# CHAPTER 2

## WHAT IS AN EVIL ALTAR?

An evil altar is a place where evil personalities summon a Christian, an unbeliever, a group of persons or even nations to assess their spiritual strength. It is done before attacking them. Intelligent occult priests do not attack a person until such a target is accessed to know his spiritual level, and therefore determine the right weapon to use. If an evil priest does not assess his target before attacking them, he may end up attacking a higher occult member and this may cause much damage or even the loss of his life in the satanic kingdom. Reckless and unintelligent occult priests may just attack anybody they see and that may become disastrous for them. All the same, it is dangerous for anybody to appear on the evil altar at all.

The fact is that as a Christian, you are not supposed to appear there at all. This is because once you appear you can be deposited for future attack; and if you do not withdraw yourself, in your weak moment, they may destroy something in your life, steal a very important thing from your life or even kill you. They can also steal one's brain, business, finance, joy, prosperity or even destroy an important organ in one's body. Again, they can remove one's heart entirely.

> *"I shall see him, but not now: I shall behold him, but not nigh: there shall come a Star out of Jacob, and a Sceptre shall rise out of Israel, and shall smite the corners of Moab, and destroy all the children of Sheth" (Numbers 24:17).*

Balaam told Balak that he would see the Israelites, but seeing them was not the ultimate thing. Balaam was a very intelligent prophet but he was defiled by the love of money, which is the root of all evil. "I shall see him but attacking him is not now", so said Balaam (Num. 24:17). This evil prophecy was fulfilled in Numbers 25:1-3, 6-9.

*"And Israel abode in Shittim, and the people began to commit whoredom with the daughters of Moab. And they called the people unto the sacrifices of their gods: and the people did eat, and bowed down to their gods. And Israel joined himself unto Baal–peor: and the anger of the LORD was kindled against Israel… And, behold, one of the children of Israel came and brought unto his brethren a Midianites woman in the sight of Moses, and in the sight of all the congregation of the children of Israel, who were weeping before the door of the tabernacle of the congregation. And when Phinehas, the son of Eleazar, the son of Aaron the priest, saw it, he rose up from among the congregation, and took a javelin in his hand; And he went after the man of Israel into the tent, and thrust both of them through, the man of Israel, and the woman through her belly. So the plague was stayed from*

*the children of Israel. And those that died in the*
*plague were twenty and four thousand"*
*(Numbers 25:1-3, 6-9).*

Once somebody appears on the evil altar, he receives extra evil luggage. Therefore, every Christian should always be on fire for the Lord so as not to appear at all on evil altar. An evil altar is a place where occult nests store information about a place, person, or thing, for evil purposes. This is a satanic information house (or evil computer). A high-ranking occult person can get any information about another person from birth to his old age. However, once a Christian knows how to withdraw things from evil altars, his life will be too hot to be controlled by any evil power. This is because his or her full identity must have been withdrawn from the satanic world.

You may be born again but all your credentials may be on the marine altar. Such a person cannot get a good job. If your marriage is on the evil later, either marriage in the physical world will be impossible or they (evil powers) will allow you to marry your enemy, their agent, through whom they will manipulate your life always. It is true that as soon as somebody is born again every condemnation is cancelled as long as such a person walks in the spirit (See Romans 8:1). However, we can see many places where Satan resisted the will of God for a man, like in the case of Daniel.

*"Then said he unto me, Fear not, Daniel: for from the first day that thou didst set thine heart to understand, and to chasten thyself before thy God, thy words were heard, and I am come for thy words. But the prince of the kingdom of Persia withstood me one and twenty days: but, lo, Michael, one of the chief princes, came to help me; and I remained there with the kings of Persia"* (Daniel 10:12-13).

If Satan can resist God, he will do more to man. Deliverance then is resisting Satan, who is sitting on our benefits (James 4:7). Therefore, if you allow the file of your life to be on an evil altar, it will be there throughout your life but to your detriment.

Satan uses ignorance to keep people away from plans and promises of God. If you therefore want to maintain your relationship with God, you have to fight. I mean that being in Christ is not enough. Christian life is full of warfare (2 Corinthians 5:17). In your warfare, fight all those old things that want to remain. Bring new things into your life. Do not stay in your father's old position as a sinner. If you are born again, then rise up and demand for your full rights. If you do not demand them through warfare prayers, Satan will not willingly surrender them to you.

Salvation is necessary; but you also need spiritual warfare. In fact, salvation and holiness qualifies a person for warfare. So what are you waiting for?

There was a sister whose father was rich but her stepmother was sitting on the man's wealth with her powerful witchcraft. During her National Youth service Corps programme, she demanded money for a mattress but her stepmother refused to approve it. As a result, this young woman was sleeping on the floor although her father was very wealthy. This sister therefore went into a spiritual exercise of praying and fasting. During that exercise, she had a revelation in which she saw a very big warehouse filled with all good things of life. Each of these items appeared in various kinds and sizes. In fact, everything that one needs in his life was there. At that stage, an angel came down from heaven and forced the strongman blocking the warehouse out of the door. The angel then asked the sister what she needed from the warehouse and she pointed at a small sized mattress. The angel of God went in, brought out exactly that size, and gave it to her. She received the mattress from the angel and woke up.

After a while, she received a phone Call from her father who requested to know what she needed. Again, this sister only demanded a small mattress; and the father sent exactly the amount of money she requested as the cost of the small mattress. When she saw me, she gave the "testimony". That warehouse which contained every good thing in life belonged to her. That was her personal warehouse but she came to where her blessings were and claimed only a small mattress. Take the following Prayer Points:

1.  By faith, I enter into my life's warehouse, in the name of Jesus.

2.  Any strongman blocking me from my warehouse, die, in the name of Jesus.

3.  O Lord, command your angels to release all my blessings to me, in the name of Jesus.

4.  You, my destiny, jump out of evil prisons, in the name of Jesus.

5.      Every evil padlock locking my warehouse, break
        to pieces, in the name of Jesus.


An evil altar is a place where real lives are deposited. A
person can be alive, but he or she is only carrying a fake
life about; a life that every good thing of life has deserted.
Once a person's real life is deposited on an evil altar, his
or her life will become miserable. Failure will be his
portion and nobody will be interested in helping that
person. His dream life will be a confused one. He will be
in this world physically but his spiritual life will be terribly
sick. He may be intelligent and prosperous in the world of
darkness but a failure in this physical world. In his dreams,
he may own the best of cars, and see himself comfortable
in the spirit world but here, he will be mad (or half mad).

An evil altar is a place of sacrifice. This includes evil
sacrifice of one's time in gossiping and in committing
other sins. Any place where blood is shed is an evil altar.
Any name that is mentioned there is in danger and
therefore needs to be called out from there. Anywhere that
blood is demanded today for sacrifice is an evil altar. The
only blood sacrifice recognized by the Almighty God

today is the blood of Jesus, which was shed on the Cross of Calvary.

> *"By so much was Jesus made a surety of a better testament. herefore he is able also to save them to the uttermost that come unto God by him, seeing he ever liveth to make intercession for them... Who needeth not daily, as those high priests, to offer up sacrifice, first for his own sins, and then for the people's: for this he did once, when he offered up himself"* (<u>Hebrews 7:22, 25, 27</u>).

Jesus is the end of the law because He fulfilled the law.

An evil altar is a place where blood is shed and a place where blood cries. It is a place of slaughter.

> *"And Balaam said unto Balak, Build me here seven altars, and prepare me here seven oxen and seven rams. And Balak did as Balaam had spoken; and Balak and Balaam offered on every altar a bullock and a ram... And Balak said unto*

*him, Come, I pray thee, with me unto another place, from whence thou mayest see them: thou shalt see but the utmost part of them, and shalt not see them all: and curse me them from thence. And he brought him into the field of Zophim, to the top of Pisgah, and built seven altars, and offered a bullock and a ram on every altar... <sup>27</sup>And Balak said unto Balaam, Come, I pray thee, I will bring thee unto another place; peradventure it will please God that thou mayest curse me them from thence. <sup>28</sup>And Balak brought Balaam unto the top of Peor, that looketh toward Jeshimon. <sup>29</sup>And Balaam said unto Balak, Build me here seven altars, and prepare me here seven bullocks and seven rams. <sup>30</sup>And Balak did as Balaam had said, and offered a bullock and a ram on every altar"* (Numbers 23:1-2, 13-14, 27-30).

There were two towns involved in a land dispute. Each of them was consulting occult powers to be able to win the battle. They were both making sacrifices with different types of animals. They fought for many years but none of these towns could win the war and own the land. One day, a native doctor told one of the warring communities that if it wanted to possess the land fully and perpetually, it should bring a baby of a few hours of age for sacrifice. The young men of one of the communities then laid ambush on the disputed land. When they saw a pregnant woman from the other community, they kidnapped and carried her on their shoulders to their town. They then invited the native doctor who killed the woman, brought out the baby in her womb, and used it for sacrifice for that community. From that day, the other community withdrew from the dispute. In addition, up until today, that town, which killed a pregnant woman, remains the owner of the land. There was a similar story in the Bible (see 2 Kings 3:26-27).

> *"And when the king of Moab saw that the battle was too sore for him, he took with him seven hundred men that drew swords, to break through even unto the king of Edom: but they could not. Then he took his eldest son that should have reigned in his stead, and offered him for a burnt offering upon the wall. And there was great indignation against Israel: and they departed*

*from him, and returned to their own land" (2*
*Kings 3:26-27).*

The matter becomes more serious when the sacrifice is made against a person using unclean animals like a vulture, tortoise, lion or any other dangerous animals. Tortoise sacrifice against the person makes his or her life progress very slowly. When a vulture is used, it brings poverty and premature death and makes the person's life useless. The blood of those animals on the evil altar constantly cries out inviting demons to attack the people whom the sacrifices were performed against. In addition, unless serious prayers of deliverance from evil altars are done, the blood never ceases to cry against the person concerned. The blood of a higher animal can" swallow" the voice of another lesser blood sacrifice. The cry of blood can be renewed by another sacrifice. As soon as it is done, calamity revisits the person or persons the sacrifice made against.

There are stiff competitions in the occult work of blood sacrifice. The highest of all blood sacrifice is when a human being is involved. The cry of human blood has always attracted God's attention from time immemorial

(Exodus 3:7-8). The blood of innocent people/children in Egypt attracted God and He came down and dealt with Pharaoh and his people (Exodus 1:15-16). Almost every space in Egypt was polluted by blood. In Revelation 6:9-10, blood cries for revenge and anywhere blood is shed becomes an evil altar. A drop of innocent blood in a particular portion of land pollutes the land. The blood of Abel disturbed God until He came down for revenge against Cain (Genesis 4:10). All that a son says when he/she is dying is very important. It is dangerous and of disastrous consequences when his/her words are negative. The only sacrifice acceptable to God is the renewal of the one He offered Himself by faith.

*"But Christ being come an high priest of good things to come, by a greater and more perfect tabernacle, not made with hands, that is to say, not of this building; Neither by the blood of goats and calves, but by his own blood he entered in once into the holy place, having obtained eternal redemption for us. For if the blood of bulls and of goats, and the ashes of an heifer sprinkling the unclean, sanctifieth to the purifying of the flesh: How much more shall the blood of Christ, who*

*through the eternal Spirit offered himself without spot to God, purge your conscience from dead works to serve the living God? And for this cause he is the mediator of the new testament, that by means of death, for the redemption of the transgressions that were under the first testament, they which are called might receive the promise of eternal inheritance" (<u>Hebrews 9:11-15</u>).*

This is the only sacrifice, if applied in faith that attracts divine favor. The blood of Jesus can stop the cry of all human and animal sacrifices made by occult people against you just in a moment of time. Once these evil sacrifices hear the voice of the blood of Jesus, all their power against you will receive immediate termination. Even if you are the most notorious armed robber or the worst murderer, as long as you are determined to follow Jesus at all costs, no power can touch you. Remember the thief on the cross (Luke 23:39, 43).

## THE SPEAKING BLOOD

*"And to Jesus the mediator of the new covenant, and to the blood of sprinkling, that speaketh better things than that of Abel"* (Hebrew 12:24).

This was the blood that spoke to three thousand people on the Pentecost Day, and they were pricked in their hearts. Those who beat and murdered Jesus asked the greatest question of their lives, "What shall we do?" (Acts 2:37). This blood healed a man who was born crippled, and had stayed forty years in that condition. By His stripes, the man was healed (Acts 3:67).

Through faith in this blood a miracle took place and five thousand sinners without hope were fed with the word of God and they all repented and escaped hell (Acts 4:1-4). This was the blood that confronted many sick people, saved them from their sins, and healed their sicknesses as recorded in the scriptures (Acts 5:12-16). This was the blood that spoke to the prison gates through an angel and Peter was delivered (Acts 12:6-10). This was the blood that spoke to death, and Hutches, who was dead, escaped the grip of death (Acts 20:9-12).

This was the blood that silenced all the marine voices, the violence of the queen of the coast in the high sea, for Apostle Paul's sake. This blood defeated and disgraced the south wind and confronted the tempestuous wind called, Euroclydon, which was established in a marine crossroads altar in the high sea against Paul.

*"And when the south wind blew softly, supposing that they had obtained their purpose, loosing thence, they sailed close by Crete. But not long after there arose against it a tempestuous wind, called Euroclydon. And when the ship was caught, and could not bear up into the wind, we let her drive. And running under a certain island which is called Clauda, we had much work to come by the boat: [17]Which when they had taken up, they used helps, undergirding the ship; and, fearing lest they should fall into the quicksands, strake sail, and so were driven" (Acts 27:13-17).*

The voice of this blood put to shame, the powers that bewitched a whole city; and silenced the voice of the highest wizard of his generation. Thus, he delivered people who had for a very long time been under bewitchment (Acts 8:5-12).

This blood (of Jesus) can speak you out of barrenness, incurable diseases, poverty, late marriage, joblessness, failure, and all negativities of life. This was the ever-speaking blood that out speaks the blood of Abel. Once the blood of Jesus Christ speaks, every other voice will give up.

A sister had a problem getting married. Each time a brother proposed to her, a man would appear to her in a dream and say: "For better, for worse, you are married; why do you want to marry again?" The next day, the brother would become discouraged, and that would be the end of proposal. She started deliverance session, she saw herself locked up in the dream within an old house. This sister said that she was the only person in that dream who had new flesh, as all the others were like skeletons.

According to her, she heard a knock on the door and a voice of a man. Immediately, the security guard asked him who he was and what he came for. She said that at that juncture, the man who knocked mentioned her name as the person he came to take away from there. Nevertheless, the security guard laughed and stated: "It is not possible because nobody has ever come in here and was let go."

The sister went further to say that the man quoted some portions of the scripture and claimed that she was a Christian. The security guard agreed but insisted that none of their captives there had ever been allowed to go. As the argument continued, the evil power at the gate reluctantly opened the door and allowed her to go. While the two of them were going away from that place, she woke up. Miraculously, within next few days, a brother came, made a marriage proposal to her, and eventually married her. The blood of Jesus can speak you out of every problem or calamity. No blood of all evil sacrifices put together can challenge the precious blood of our Redeemer, Jesus Christ.

*"He that despised Moses' law died without mercy under two or three witnesses: Of how much sorer punishment, suppose ye, shall he be thought worthy, who hath trodden underfoot the Son of God, and hath counted the blood of the covenant, where with he was sanctified, an unholy thing, and hath done despite unto the Spirit of grace?*

*For we know him that hath said, Vengeance belongeth unto me, I will recompense, saith the Lord. And again, The Lord shall judge his people. It is a fearful thing to fall into the hands of the living God" (Hebrew 10:28-31).*

An evil altar is a spiritual dining table where evil spirits gather to eat. If you have ever been involved in any blood sacrifice, you have built an evil table, where Satan can feed. You need to destroy it and build another altar i.e. a good altar "unto God." If your ancestors or your enemies have built an evil altar against you, you need to destroy it and build another one with the blood of Jesus.

*"And it came to pass the same night, that the LORD said unto him, Take thy father's young bullock, even the second bullock of seven years old, and throw down the altar of Baal that thy father hath, and cut down the grove that is by it: And build an altar unto the LORD thy God upon the top of this rock, in the ordered place, and take the second bullock, and offer a burnt*

*sacrifice with the wood of the grove which thou*
*shalt cut down" (Judges 6:25-26).*

An evil altar is a place of evil exchange. This is what we call evil transfer altar. There have been instances of transfers of marriages, transfers of sexes - males to females - and change of the human brain to that of a goat. Destinies can also be transferred.

An evil altar is a place of contact with a wicked spirits.

*"And, behold, there came a man of God out of*
*Judah by the word of the LORD unto Beth–el:*
*and Jeroboam stood by the altar to burn*
*incense. And he cried against the altar in the*
*word of the LORD, and said, O altar, altar, thus*
*saith the LORD; Behold, a child shall be born*
*unto the house of David, Josiah by name; and*
*upon thee shall he offer the priests of the high*
*places that burn incense upon thee, and men's*
*bones shall be burnt upon thee. And he gave a*
*sign the same day, saying, This is the sign which*
*the LORD hath spoken; Behold, the altar shall be*
*rent, and the ashes that are upon it shall be*

*poured out. And it came to pass, when king Jeroboam heard the saying of the man of God, which had cried against the altar in Beth–el, that he put forth his hand from the altar, saying, lay hold on him. And his hand, which he put forth against him, dried up, so that he could not pull it in again to him. The altar also was rent, and the ashes poured out from the altar, according to the sign which the man of God had given by the word of the LORD"* (*1 Kings 13:1-5*).

This was the spirit, which followed the young prophet in the Bible and this is the spirit that is destroying many great ministers toady. The same spirit destroyed Balaam. This was the spirit that was defeated in Egypt and at the Red Sea but he (the wicked spirit) waited for Moses at the gate of Canaan. (See Deuteronomy 32:48-52). This kind of spirit can allow a person to be the greatest miracle worker. Nevertheless, since a sin can overcome such a person, he may not mind leaving; but will just wait for him at the gate of heaven, to prevent him from entering. Holiness is no other thing than the absence of sin. The presence of sin in the life of a person is the worst thing that can happen to such a person (see Hebrews 12:1-2).

An evil altar is a place of spiritual fellowship with unclean spirits. When you see yourself with sinners in a dream, you are having a fellowship with evil spirits on evil altars. When you are having sex in a dream, you are fellowshipping with unclean spirits. Any time you see yourself eating in a dream or drinking, you are, having fellowship with unclean spirits. Dreams that bring terrible fears are from the evil altars of Satan; and such dreams can afflict a person with incurable sickness. The purpose of satanic dreams from evil altars is to steal, kill, and destroy. It is also to confuse and darken our vision. Any dream that does not agree with the teachings of the scriptures is from the evil altar.

When you see yourself naked in a dream, it is to expose you to shame. The playing of Ludo or draughts in a dream is a manipulation from the evil altar. Seeing your grandparents (your ancestors) in your dreams is a linkage to ancestral evils. Wearing earrings or any other form of jewellery in a dream is an indication that evil powers want to turn the person concerned to a slave. When you see yourself carrying a load in a dream, it means that many problems have been assigned to you from the evil altars. Seeing snails in a dream or counting cowries, means slow progress for you and it also has the evil altar as its source.

Evil powers use dreams to bring somebody into fellowship with unclean spirits on satanic altars, i.e. evil altars. Evil altars can be said to be the source of every problem in this life. An evil altar is a place of evil covenants. Any place evil discussions and agreements are reached is an evil altar. Moreover, we need deliverance from that place. An evil altar is a place of evil deliberations, evil decisions, and evil actions. An evil altar is a place where evil actions commence.

# PRAYER POINTS

1. Mistakes; possess any evil altar priest that will call my name for evil, in the name of Jesus.

2. Any mistake that will promote me; cleave upon my enemies, in the name of Jesus.

3. Any man, woman, or power that wants to summon me to evil altars; summon yourself and destroy yourself, in name of Jesus.

4. Any programme going on any evil altar must favor me by fire, in the name of Jesus.

5. Any opposition established against me in the evil altar; oppose my opposers, in the name of Jesus.

6. Any assessment against me on any evil altar must be to my favor, in the name of Jesus.

7. If anything will appear at all on the evil altar when I am called, let it be the blood of Jesus, in the name of Jesus.

8. Let the power of evil altars destroy their users, in the name of Jesus.

9. Fire of God; damage the damagers on the evil altars, in the name of Jesus.

10. If I must be dragged to the evil altar, let the fourth man that helped Shedrach, Meshach and Abednego help me, in the name of Jesus.

11. Any power that has deposited me on the evil altar for future attack; release me and die, in the name of Jesus.

12. Anything the enemy has stolen from me on the evil altar, I recover you now, in the name of Jesus.

13. Every problem in my life from the evil altars; be converted to my promotion, in the name of Jesus.

14. Every hope of the enemy against me on the evil altar; be disappointed, in the name of Jesus.

15. Any intelligent evil altar priest prophesying evil against me; die with failure, in the name of Jesus.

16. Silver and gold will not destroy me, in the name of Jesus.

17. Let the fire of God in me scatter every evil altar trying to pin me down, in the name of Jesus.

18. Any luggage in my life from the evil altar; you that evil priest, come and carry them by force now, in the name of Jesus.

19. You my enemies on the land, sea, and earth; begin to collect my problems until they are finished, in the name of Jesus.

20. Every priest working against me; receive wrong information concerning me to promote me, in the name of Jesus.

21. If I am born again, let my situation change now for the better, in the name of Jesus.

22. Old things in my life reproaching God, don't you know that I am born again? Die, in the name of Jesus.

23. Old things in my life bringing shame to the gospel; the Lord rebuke them, in the name of Jesus.

24. Fire of God; begin to burn the old things in my life until they are no more, in the name of Jesus.

25. Satan, I resist you with the blood of Jesus; mingle with fire, in the name of Jesus.

26. Any ignorance in my life, promoting my problem; be converted by force, in the name of Jesus.

27. New things in Christ that would advance me; what are you waiting for? Possess me now, in the name of Jesus.

28. Oh Lord, give me strength for a battle that will advance me, in the name of Jesus.

29. Any warfare going on against me; known and unknown; I receive victory now, in the name of Jesus.

30. My divine warehouse; open for me by fire, in the name of Jesus.

31. I shall not suffer while things that will make me comfortable are available. I claim them now, in the name of Jesus.

32. If praying and fasting will solve my problem; Oh Lord, give me the power to fast until I overcome all my enemies in the name of Jesus.

33. Oh Lord, take me to where they are not expecting me, in the name of Jesus.

34. Devil, destroy your case file against my life and lose the case in the name of Jesus.

35. Devil, with your own hand, destroy my relationship with you in any evil altar, in the name of Jesus.

36. Devil, with your mouth, speak good things concerning me this year that will make me destroy your kingdom, in the name of Jesus.

37. Devil, cause your demons to respect me, in the name of Jesus.

38. Devil, assign your agents to carry out my instructions against yours, in the name of Jesus.

39. Satan, go and destroy what you have done in the evil altar against my home, in the name of Jesus.

40. Devil, work day and night to promote me thinking that you are destroying me, in the name of Jesus.

41. Evil priest, offer sacrifices against yourself, in the name of Jesus.

42. Bad dream, possess my Pharaoh and promote me, in the name of Jesus.

43. Let my Nebuchadnezzar enter into the bush for seven years to learn their lessons, in the name of Jesus.

44. Any prayer that will not favor me, let my enemy forget it, in the name of Jesus.

45. Forces of darkness, release me into holiness and prosperity approved by God, in the name of Jesus.

46. Evil altars' security personnel; release all your captives by compulsory power from above, in the name of Jesus.

# CHAPTER 3

# KINDS OF EVIL ALTARS

## CROSSROADS ALTAR

*"And when the south wind blew softly, supposing that they had obtained their purpose, loosing thence, they sailed close by Crete. But not long after there arose against it a tempestuous wind, called Euroclydon. And when the ship was caught, and could not bear up into the wind, we let her drive" (Acts 27:13-15).*

Eurodydon is an ancient term for an eastern storm, which modern people call levanter, a typhoon, whirlwind or hurricane, blowing in all directions. A crossroad altar is therefore an imitation of the cross of Calvary. Satan imitates whatever God does. The crossroad altar can be established anywhere, in the air, stream, river, sea, ocean, inside a building, etc. It could be visible or invisible, in a four-corner path or road. It is an attack from the extreme parts of the four cardinal points; namely: North, South, East, and West. If you have lived in most African villages, you must have observed that there is always a sacrifice made at four corner paths or roads. The purpose is to invoke and invite demons from the extreme parts of the world, and feed them to deliberate and take decisions as to who to destroy among men.

They destroy human beings, places, and things.

It is a place where demons come together for refreshment courses, and declare their identity and area of specialization. Those who are witches and wizards are gathered. Demons in charge of madness, poverty, late marriages, failure, etc., will be singled out for evil assignments against humanity, places and things.

The enemy has indeed made the world a centre of battle. Therefore, anybody who does not engage himself in the battle of this life will be defeated even without knowing it. The rich man in the book of Luke chapter sixteen, was defeated but he was not aware of it (Luke 16:19-31).

There are many ministers of God who have been defeated by these evil powers but they are yet to know it. Physical prosperity and praises from men, assuring you that you are a good man of God are not enough. You have to examine your life in the light of the word of God - the Holy Bible. The rich man was clothed in purple and fine linen and fed sumptuously every day. When the word of God said every day, He means every day. Every day of the rich man's life was spent without pain, sickness or lack.

Any prosperity without total freedom from sin and faith in Christ Jesus is deceit of the highest order. True prosperity should be balanced. It should embrace the various aspects of one's life. You can be a king receiving favors from everywhere. You may have been basing your actions on what men say about you. There was a king like that in the Bible, a prince who inherited kingship. He went to the best university in his days and graduated with the best grade possible. He ruled the world then, which had about one hundred and twenty seven provinces. He controlled kings, governors, princes, captains, counsellors, airways and all men in the world then. However, he still failed when he was scaled in divine standards. Whatever you are or have, amounts to nothing without divine approval.

> *"And this is the writing that was written, MENE, MENE, TEKEL, UPHARSIN. This is the interpretation of the thing: MENE; God hath numbered thy kingdom, and finished it. TEKEL; Thou art weighed in the balances, and art found wanting. PERES; Thy kingdom is divided, and given to the Medes and Persians" (Daniel 5:25-28).*

The spirits from crossroads altars are the most intelligent. They are mixed up (demons) from all satanic departments with the intention to destroy creation. They can bombard a person with evil or good for the purpose of eventual destruction. They have wealth, protection, prosperity, power, position, and other things that a man needs, but Christ. They can promote a person to extreme; and at the height of it all, the person will fall to the extreme too (Ezekiel 28:11, 19). These were the spirits, which destroyed Lot's wife. They also destroyed Pharaoh. They were the spirits that also killed Nadab and Abihu (Leviticus 10:1-7). They were the spirits that destroyed Dathan, Korah, Abiram, and all the renowned men of Israel, some of whom were buried alive. They were the spirits that used Balak to offer promises to Balaam and he undertook an assignment against God's people. They are the spirits that killed Achan with covetousness. These same spirits killed Samson in a strange land. They are the kind of evil altar spirits that promoted the giant, Goliath; gave him an extremely intimidating physique, and an evil tongue to blaspheme God. In addition, in the midst of his pride, a small boy at the height of shame and humiliation destroyed him. Demons from crossroads altars have done and are still doing havoc in the lives of men. The spirit from artificial crossroads altars finished Judas Iscariot.

## TREE ALTAR

*"But of the tree of the knowledge of good and evil, thou shalt not eat of it: for in the day that thou eatest thereof thou shalt surely die"* (Genesis 2:17).

In many African states today, demons have possessed many trees. Many trees are being worshipped today as gods. In my town, there was a time a tree fell down and later stood up again. An apple tree in a particular community, which was being worshipped normally, donated apple fruits to its visitors. Once you get there, one of the fruit will fall for you, and if more than one person went there at once, this apple tree would donate one apple to each person. The lives of people are dedicated to trees in many parts of the world today. In some parts of eastern Nigeria, people worship trees. The Igbo for instance, worship trees like *ngwu*, *ogbu*, *ogirisi* and *oji* as gods. A child could be dedicated to a tree altar before conception or, while it is still in the womb. Some tree altars also demand human sacrifice.

## WALL ALTAR

*"And when the king of Moab saw that the battle was too sore for him, he took with him seven hundred men that drew swords, to break through even unto the king of Edom: but they could not. Then he took his eldest son that should have reigned in his stead, and offered him for a burnt*

*offering upon the wall. And there was great indignation against Israel: and they departed from him, and returned to their own land" (2 Kings 3:26-27).*

The god of the Moabites lived inside walls. The god of the Moabites usually demanded for human sacrifice. Witches and wizards travel through walls. People, who place their legs on the walls while sleeping, travel through those walls for evil meetings and actions.

Many people in different parts of the world have walls as their altars. Therefore, a wall can serve as an evil altar to somebody, somewhere, even today.

## ROCK ALTAR

In different parts of the world, people gather stones or go to where there are natural rocks to offer sacrifice to the gods in those rock altars. I know somewhere in a country where five communities have a common rock altar, which is made up of five big stones. This altar is located in one of these five communities. These five big towns are ruled according to the dictates and influences of the evil spirits in the "naturally installed" rock altar.

Top government officials and prominent men in this nation, go to where this rock altar is located to offer sacrifice and obtain "political power and protection." It was at this location that an apple tree that used to entertain its guests with one apple per person bowed unto God Almighty, who has uprooted the evil tree. The tree fell from the roots when believers there were dedicating a baby boy to God and were ascribing authority, power and glory to God Almighty while renouncing and declaring the rock altar there as powerless.

# EVIDENCE OF CAPTIVITY OF EVIL ALTARS

## HUMAN ALTARS DREAMS

Sometime ago, a particular undergraduate was delayed from graduating for many years. He was unable to pass a particular course. He found out that each time the examination is coming, a particular woman in his family would just appear to him in the dream and he would end up not passing the examination.

A pastor was told that his younger sister was mad. On getting home, he discovered that one occult man from the village was manipulating the sister's brain. The girl was prayed for and she recovered from the mental sickness and brought all her religious books to be burnt. The pastor later went to the occult man and warned him not to inflict his sister again. The occult man simply looked straight into the eyes of the pastor and kept quiet. The pastor left and that was the beginning of his problems. In the night of that day, the pastor was shot in the tip of his fingers and he woke up from his sleep very mad. He was then rushed to the church. Thanks to God that he was delivered. That was an attack from the evil human altar.

A particular man was served with a quit notice. He was given an ultimatum to quite his apartment within seven days. Somehow, he appealed against it through a lawyer. His property owner who had a human evil altar became angry and boasted that he would deal with him. That night, as the man was sleeping, he saw himself lifted very high into the sky. His property owner then cut off his head with a knife. While his head was going up, the other part of his body was coming down to the earth.

At that juncture, he shouted: "Blood of Jesus!" Immediately, his head and body came together again. The property owner told him to agree that he had died but he confessed: "NO! How can I agree that I am dead?" This happened three times before the brother woke up but noticed that his heart was no longer there. He then prayed earnestly and called back his departed heart and life already arrested by his (human evil altar) property owner.

## FAMILY SHRINE ALTAR DREAMS

When you dream about your place of birth repeatedly, it is an indication that there is an evil altar there, which has enslaved you. Your parents must have dedicated you to the evil powers there and dreaming like that means that these evil powers are calling you back to reduce you to the level of your ancestors or even below. Some demand the renewal of ancestral agreements or Sacrifice, which you may not even know anything about. Whenever you dream of a particular place always, there is an altar there fighting you. To some people, it is the school they left many years ago that they always dream of. To some it may be where they lived before, their business location and places they may not know. Somehow, part of them was taken there for sacrifice. In that case, you need to say serious prayers in order to withdraw your life, or anything representing you there.

## UNPROFITABLE TENANTS

It is observed that immediately some people move into a house, failure set in. They will lose valuable property, or become victims of sickness, disease, death, and loss of everything good. Some property owners usually enter into a covenant with the devil before building their houses, or even have the houses dedicated to demons. Moreover, unless the tenants are able to stop the crying blood, and establish a new covenant after destroying the old one, they may not succeed in that house.

An incident took place some time ago between a woman and an *okada* man (a commercial motorcyclist). They agreed that the fare would be ten Naira. When the woman got to her destination, she gave the man twenty naira. Instead of giving the woman her balance of ten naira, the *okada* man dropped it on the ground for her to pick. Nevertheless, the woman refused to pick it up. As the argument continued, a crowd gathered and the *okada* man was compelled to give the woman her balance since the woman did not drop money for him to pick. The man brought out another ten naira from his pocket and gave to the woman.

However, as he was about to go, the crowd held him and forced him to pick the ten naira he dropped on the ground; and immediately the man picked it, he disappeared. Some people who knew him gathered and went to his house and found him sitting inside his wardrobe and different types of Nigerian currency notes were being vomited by him. That was exactly what he wanted the woman passenger to be doing for him, i.e. to stay in his wardrobe and vomit money for him always.

What would you call that kind of wardrobe? Certainly, it is an evil altar. Many houses have been converted to evil altars today. We have altars in many kitchens. Once you eat food cooked in that kind of kitchen, your life will become contaminated, and some ugly dreams will start to occur in your life. We need to rededicate our houses to the Lord after casting out and destroying the old altars.

*"See, I have this day set thee over the nations and over the kingdoms, to root out, and to pull down, and to destroy, and to throw down, to build, and to plant" (Jeremiah 1:10).*

## SPIRITUAL BACKWARDNESS

When you are experiencing a "rise and fall" in your spiritual life like in prayer, fasting, service to God, etc., there is an altar against you. Some time ago, I arrived at a particular place for ministration and I discovered that each night before the deliverance each week, I always fought, ate, or did one dirty thing or another in a dream. In addition, that was aimed at reducing my spiritual life before the morning of deliverance. Once that was done, I would not minister effectively that week. After some time, I focused my prayers on the altars in charge of spiritual defilement and the Lord delivered me. Anything that happens to reduce your zeal, prayers, and spiritual ability, is from evil altars. When you find out that, you cannot pray in a particular place there is an evil altar there. When you cannot function effectively in a particular place, an altar is dealing with you.

## COMPULSORY PROBLEMS

These are problems that are seasonal or that come at a time when you are about to achieve a goal. It can be memory failure when you are in need of information, compulsory stealing, errors, etc. A particular student was advised to go through a series of prayers, which we call deliverance. According to her, she wanted to undergo the deliverance but owing to her academic work - many resist and carry-overs, she decided to concentrate on her studies.

In the evening of the day preceding her main examinations, she came to my office for prayers. Her specific prayer point was for her to be led by God to the topics that would come out the following day. We prayed and the Lord did exactly that - her prayer was answered. That morning of the examination, when she read the question paper, she became very happy and confident of a very good result, since all she had studied were the things on which the questions were centered. Nevertheless, immediately she wanted to start writing, she forgot all the ideas and became confused.

Some other people would get to a place only when those that are supposed to help them have left there or are not in the mood to render any help to them. Once it is time for their success, a reshuffle will take place and the person that is determined to help them will be reassigned. Such people will be having constant problems that will repeatedly bring them into failures. Those who are receiving attacks from evil altars will be seeing things, which others do not see. They will be having business disappointments and failure. There will be amputated finances; and it will be as if the whole world is against such people. Evil altars close good doors against some people and open the doors of afflictions, sicknesses, and diseases to them.

# PRAYER POINTS

## WAR AGAINST AGGRESSIVE EVIL ALTARS

1.  Demons in the evil altars assigned against my life; kill yourselves with your own weapon, in the name of Jesus.

2.  Aggressive evil altar priests; scatter your altars and die, in the name of Jesus.

3.  Crossroad altars; refuse to cooperate with my enemies, in the name, of Jesus.

4.  As from today, I destroy evil invitations in the evil altars against my life, in the name of Jesus.

5.  I block the entrance gates of evil altars into my destiny, in the name of Jesus.

6.  Evil refreshments in the evil altars; cease, in the name of Jesus.

7.  Evil refreshments in the evil altars; take your house away from my existence, in the name of Jesus.

8.  Any evil tree, harboring demons against me; dry up from the root, in the name of Jesus.

9.  My destiny, come out from the rock altars of darkness, in the name of Jesus.

10. Evil deposits in my life from the evil altars; come out and enter no more, in the name of Jesus.

11. Any masquerade or snake, attacking my life from the evil altars; die and die again, in the name of Jesus.

12. Any satanic law enforcement agent in my dream; go and arrest your sender, in the name of Jesus.

13. My property owner will not swallow my destiny, in the name of Jesus.

14. Any evil covenant existing in the place where I am living now and where I lived; break and release me, in the name of Jesus.

15. Any power following me about from the places I have been to before; go back to your sender, in the name of Jesus.

16. Any power attacking my life because of my evil relationships in the past; go back to your sender, in the name of Jesus.

17. Any power troubling me from any evil foundation; lose your hold on my life, in the name of Jesus.

18. Any evil altar demon that has vowed to destroy my prayer life; die with your priests, in the name of Jesus.

19. You the guerrillas of anointing in this land; I am not your candidate; forsake me by fire, in the name of Jesus.

20. I shall not lose my job because I am living in this house, in the name of Jesus.

21. Every compulsory problem in my life; die without mercy, in the name of Jesus.

22. Oh Lord, pull me out from stubborn altars that have vowed to render me useless, in the name of Jesus.

23. My miracles, what are you waiting for? Manifest now, in the name of Jesus.

24. My brain, think aright for I am delivered, in the name of Jesus.

25. My helpers, you cannot forget me; help me by fire, in the name of Jesus.

26. Not every disappointment is a blessing; I refuse to disappoint God, in the name of Jesus.

27.    Fire of death, burning me from the evil altar; disappear by force, in the name of Jesus.

28.    Evil murderers, turn your weapons against yourselves immediately, in the name of Jesus:

29.    Any generational curse in my life with stubborn weapons; die, in the name of Jesus.

30.    My life, jump out from the cauldron of witchcraft forever and ever, in the name of Jesus.

31.    Any congregation of demons against me; scatter, in the name of Jesus.

32.    Witches gathered on my right hand; wizards gathered on my left hand; begin to fight against yourselves, in the name of Jesus.

33.    Anything I owe to evil powers, blood of Jesus, pay for me now, in the name of Jesus.

34.    Hell fire, collect your problems in my life and go forever, in the name of Jesus.

35.    Effect of the strange hands that have touched me before; disappear, in the name of Jesus.

36.    Full deliverance; begin to take place in my life without hindrance, in the name of Jesus.

37.     Local and international demons from evil altars gathering against me; scatter, in the name of Jesus.

38.     Satanic embassies refuse to issue visas to demons into my life from today, in the name of Jesus.

39.     Fasting, praying, incantations and bewitchment will fail my enemy forever and ever, in the name of Jesus.

40.     I refuse to surrender to Satan and all his stubborn associates. They will surrender to me, in the name of Jesus.

# WAR AGAINST TREE ALTARS

1. I pull down every tree altar standing for my sake, in the name of Jesus.

2. I set ablaze every tree altar representing me, in the name of Jesus.

3. Any broom representing tree altars in my life; catch fire and burn, in the name of Jesus.

4. Any tree altars having any area of my life; vomit it and die, in the name of Jesus.

5. I lay the axe of fire on the tree altar of my family, in the name of Jesus.

6. Every covenant, binding me to tree altars; break, in the name of Jesus.

7. I release the spirit of destruction upon all stubborn tree altars in charge of my life, in the name of Jesus.

8. My soul, come out from an evil tree, in the name of Jesus.

9. I withdraw my money from every tree altar, in the name of Jesus,

10. I withdraw my health from every tree altar, in the name of Jesus.

11. I withdraw my virtue from the tree altar, in the name of Jesus.

12. I war against any tree altar in my life, in the name of Jesus.

13. Problems in my life, caused by tree altars; die, in the name of Jesus.

14. Whether the devil likes it or not, I must get out of tree altars, in the name of Jesus.

15. Tree altars of my ancestors; die, in the name of Jesus.

16. (Lay your right hand on your chest and pray like this) Every application of tree altars; stop by force, in the name of Jesus.

17. Every tree altar of witches in my compound; fall down and die, in the name of Jesus.

18. Every tree idol in my compound; fall down and die, in the name of Jesus.

19. I withdraw every sacrifice given to tree altars on my behalf, in the name of Jesus.

# HUMAN ALTARS

1.  Let the fire of God fall upon every human altar fashioned against me, in the name of Jesus.

2.  Every human altar, drinking my blood; be bound, in the name of Jesus.

3.  I break and destroy every human altar working against my life, in the name of Jesus.

4.  Let the strength of the human altar in my family be broken, in the name of Jesus.

5.  I withdraw by fire everything programmed into the heavenlies against me on human altars, in the name of Jesus.

6.  I command every human altar constructing wickedness against me: Be broken, in the name of Jesus!

7.  Any human altar, saying no to the will of God for my life; die, in the name of Jesus.

8.  Any human altar, handing me over to evil traders; fall down and die, in the name of Jesus.

9.      Any human altar, claiming to be almighty in my family; go into the bush according to the order of Nebuchadnezzar, in the name of Jesus.

10.     Every human altar, cursing my life; be silenced by fire by force in the name of Jesus.

11.     Lord, release your wrath on any human altar standing in my way to Canaan Land, in the name of Jesus.

12.     Lord, raise your indignation against every human altar gathered for my sake, in the name of Jesus.

13.     Let the way of the human altars assigned to any department of my life; perish, in the name of Jesus.

14.     Lord Jesus, laugh all human altars that are against me to scorn, in the name of Jesus.

15.     Lord, break every human altar with the rod of iron, in the name of Jesus.

16.     Lord, break the teeth of the human altars biting my life in the name of Jesus.

17.     Let every human altar, troubling my life be troubled beyond measure, in the name of Jesus.

18.     Every human altar, taking counsel against my life; fall by your own counsel, in the name of Jesus.

19.  Arise, O Lord, in your anger, and lift up yourself because of the rage of human altars against my life, in the name of Jesus.

20.  Lord, let the wickedness of the human altars against my life come to an end, in the name of Jesus.

# CHAPTER 4

## OPEN EVIL GATES

In all generations, the gate of hell is everywhere evil altars are established. That is where enemies are raised and trained against God and His people. The easiest way to open doors to Satan is through sin. Any sacrifice made to honor Satan is a gate of hell. Adam and Eve opened the gate to Satan when they discussed, obeyed, and ate the forbidden fruit (Genesis 3:6).

Lamech opened an evil gate to his life and family when he committed murder and got Cain's reward seventy times seven folds (Genesis 4:23-24; 11-12). The sons of God opened an evil gate with their eyes when they began to choose their wives by sight. They were corrupted and they became violent. That was why God destroyed the world with water then.

The same gate was opened when Ham looked on his father's nakedness (Genesis 9:21-22). The herdsmen of Abraham and Lot opened an evil gate that separated the two brothers when they allowed the spirit of strife to enter their camp. Sarai opened an evil gate when she became impatient and gave her house cleaner to her husband and she was later despised by the same house cleaner. Lot and his two daughters opened an evil gate when they became drunk and committed the worst immorality that produced Ammon and Moab, the troublers of Israel, even to date (Genesis 19:30-38). Esau, the first of the twin sons of his father, Isaac, opened an evil gate for himself and his descendants when he failed to control his appetite and tongue, thereby selling his birthright.

*"Lest there be any fornicator, or profane person, as Esau, who for one morsel of meat sold his birthright. For ye know how that afterward,*

*when he would have inherited the blessing, he*
*was rejected: for he found no place of*
*repentance, though he sought it carefully with*
*tears" (Hebrews 12:16-17).*

Shechem opened an evil gate when he defiled Dina, the daughter of Jacob, which brought about his death and the death of all the males, and the destruction of all their property.

*"And Dinah the daughter of Leah, which she*
*bare unto Jacob, went out to see the daughters of*
*the land. And when Shechem the son of Hamor*
*the Hivite, prince of the country, saw her, he took*
*her, and lay with her, and defiled her. And his*
*soul clave unto Dinah the daughter of Jacob, and*
*he loved the damsel, and spake kindly unto the*
*damsel. And Shechem spake unto his father*
*Hamor, saying, Get me this damsel to wife. And*
*Jacob heard that he had defiled Dinah his*
*daughter: now his sons were with his cattle in the*
*field: and Jacob held his peace until they were*
*come... And it came to pass on the third day,*

*when they were sore, that two of the sons of*
*Jacob, Simeon and Levi, Dinah's brethren, took*
*each man his sword, and came upon the city*
*boldly, and slew all the males. And they slew*
*Hamor and Shechem his son with the edge of the*
*sword, and took Dinah out of Shechem's house,*
*and went out. The sons of Jacob came upon the*
*slain, and spoiled the city, because they had*
*defiled their sister. They took their sheep, and*
*their oxen, and their asses, and that which* was *in*
*the city, and that which* was *in the field, And all*
*their wealth, and all their little ones, and their*
*wives took they captive, and spoiled even all that*
was *in the house" (Genesis 34:1-5, 25-29).*

Joseph's brothers opened an evil gate when they hated
their brother, Joseph; envied him, conspired against him,
stripped him of his coat, sold him, and told lies to their
father, Jacob. However, all of them eventually found
themselves being ruled by Joseph - under the government
of Joseph (Genesis 42:3-20).

Aaron and the Israelites opened an evil gate and sold a
whole nation to Satan when they built and made a molten

calf as their god, which "brought them out of Egypt" (Exodus 32:1-6). Nadab and Abihu, the sons of the high priest, Aaron, opened an evil gate right inside the temples of God when they offered strange fire before the Lord (Leviticus 10:1-2). Balaam, the former true prophet of God, opened an evil gate when he lodged sinners in his house and later went with them to curse Israel (Numbers 31:15-18, 32).

Achan, the son of Carmi, the son of Zabdi, the son of Zerah, of the tribe of Judah, opened an evil gate when he took the accursed thing - the Babylonian garment, which he never enjoyed and died with his entire family (Joshua 7:1; Malachi 2:12-17). The enemies of God and the Israelites opened an evil gate together when they took God's items of silver and gold to an idol's temple and sold the people of God (Jeremiah 50:51; Joel 3:1-21).

Jehu opened an evil gate when the blood of Jezreel was found on his head thereby allowing demons to occupy his head (Hosea 1:1-5). The people of Israel opened an evil gate when they trod upon the poor, took wheat, afflicted the just, offered and accepted bribes, fasted and sang choruses in sin, etc. (Amos 5:1-27).

The people of Nineveh, controlling about one hundred and twenty-seven provinces in the world then, opened an evil gate when they became wicked (Jonah 1:1-2). The princes and prophets in Israel opened an evil gate when they became cruel, made the people to err, became perverted, built houses with blood money, passed judgment for reward, taught for hire and divined for money (Micah 3:1). God's enemies opened an evil gate when they began to contend with God, shed blood in the city, told lies, robbed, and committed whoredom (Nahum 1:1-15) The Israelites opened evil gates when they committed iniquity, became violent and committed wicked acts (Habakkuk 1:1-14).

The people of Assyria and Ethiopia opened an evil gate when they began to dwell carelessly and rejoiced in their pride (Zephaniah 2:12-15): A certain scribe, whom Jesus loved, opened an evil gate of prosperity without Christ when he preferred luxury to the preaching of the gospel (Matthew 8:19-20).

King Herod, his wife, and daughter, opened a permanent gate of destruction to Herod's family when he married his brother's wife, put John the Baptist in prison, and later beheaded him (Mark 7:17-28; Luke 3:19-20). The Pharisees, the lawyers, and the Sanhedrin opened evil gates to themselves and Israel when they rejected the counsel of God (John 3:19-20). Pilate opened an evil gate to himself and his family when he rejected good counsel from his wife, sat down to judge his own Creator; - the Lord Jesus - scourged Him, and compromised with the Jews.

Ananias and Sapphira opened an evil gate of death and hell when they took the decision to lie to the Holy Ghost (Acts 5:1-11). The Corinthian Church opened an evil gate when the members began to contend among themselves, declaring their fellowship of Paul, Apollos, Cephas, or Christ (Corinthians 1:2-3, 11-17). Some people in the church at Philippi opened an evil gate when they began to preach Christ in envy, strife, contention, etc., thereby adding affliction to Paul's bond (Philippians 1:15-16). An evil gate was opened when the false brethren began to spy Paul's liberty in Christ with a view to bringing him into bondage (Galatians 2:4-10). They opened the gate of evil into the church with their love for the work of the flesh thereby hating Christ (Galatians 5:19-21).

The young widows opened an evil gate in the days of Paul and Timothy by idleness, wandering from house to house; gossiping and speaking things they ought not to speak (1Timothy 5:11-15). Alexander the coppersmith opened an evil gate when he began to challenge God's constituted authority, thereby doing much evil to Paul. He was withstanding Paul's worlds (2 Timothy 4:14-18). In 2 John, verses 9 through 12, whosoever does not abide in the doctrine of Christ is opening an evil gate. The Ephesians Christians opened an evil gate when they left their first love (Revelation 2:1, 4-7).

The believers at Pergamus opened an evil gate when they held the doctrine of Balaam and Nicolaitanes, which God hates (Revelation 2:12-17). The Thyatira Christians opened an evil gate when they allowed Jezebel, the prophetess, to lead them; preaching in the church and also to prophesy, fornicate, eat, and sacrifice to idols (Revelation 2:18-29). The Christians in Sadis opened an evil gate when they became spiritually dead without knowing it (Revelation 3:1-6). The worst type of ignorance is when one is ignorant of one's ignorance.

The Christians at Laodicea opened an evil gate when they became lukewarm; neither cold nor hot; not knowing that they were poor and wretched and in need of all things (Revelation 3:14-22). This is high-class ignorance. In the scriptures, one discovers that in the days of old, gates were made at the entrance of cities. It could be a gate by the beach, to palaces (Esther 5), rivers, temples (Acts 3), persons, etc. It could also be a house. Very important discussions were held at the city gates in the Bible days. Incantations that affected the whole city were made at the gates. Many students lose their intelligence immediately they enter into campus gates. Some people lose their occult power to other superior powers by passing through some gates. Every evil gate has security demons at the checkpoint. Some students are unknowingly marked by security demons at the evil gate to be hated by people inside the campus. That is why some students may be hated and even failed by some lecturers for no just cause.

Ignorant Christians at the evil gates lose many valuables. At prison gates, many prisoners are possessed to become hardened criminals as soon as they enter into the prison. Some occult houses make people lose their consciousness at the evil gates or the entrances of the buildings. That is why the enemy's first point of concentration during wars was the gates of cities. Most gates are shut at night.

They can be opened or shut for good or evil. A woman told me that marine spirits gave her an assignment to pull down a particular pastor in Lagos, Nigeria. According to her when she approached the pastor's office the door was physically open but spiritually locked up. In addition, being decorated with powerful demons, she could not enter with those powers. When she knocked on the door, the pastor and others in the office told her to enter but she could not due to her evil powers. She tried but could not. Moreover, when she came downstairs, she met the pastor's wife with the door of her life and office wide open both physically and spiritually. She entered and manipulated the woman who was pregnant with a very strong passion to be delivered of her baby overseas. The pastor could not persuade his wife to have the baby in Nigeria. When he could not, he decided to table it to the members of his church. According to the marine woman, she entered into one unbeliever, a cheater, who was also a member of the church council, and the proposal was rejected.

The church was divided into two parts and that was how they began to call the police and went to court. What I am saying is that sin, worldliness, and worldly amusements or pleasure can open someone's gate of life for evil (John 2:15-17). Christians should be separated from those whose affections and desires are of the world.

Pride of life is of the world, and can open someone's gate of life for evil. Carnal festivals, lust of the eyes, etc., are abominations unto God, and can open one's gate of life to every mantle of unholy desire (Song of Solomon chapter 2:15). Christians should be dead to sin, dead to the things of this world. We should set our affections in heaven and in Christ as Apostle Paul enjoins us in (Hebrews 12:1-2).

Worldly music, films, and things that cannot contribute to our Christian growth should not be named among us as saints. We as Christians should not open the gate of our lives to Satan by our conversation, dressing, pleasures and worldly enjoyment (1 Timothy 6:6-10). Our ambition should be offered to the Lord as an offering and sacrifice; a sweet-smelling savor that should not contradict God's will. To succeed as Christians, we must get rid of inordinate affection for places, things or people. Travelling to some places or getting some things must not be a do-or-die affair especially to Christians.

# PRAYER POINTS

## VICTORY OVER SIN

1.   I break the yoke of sin in my life, in the name of Jesus.

2.   I release myself from any inherited bondage of sin, in the name of Jesus.

3.   Let the blood of Jesus flush out every sinful nature in my family members, in the name of Jesus,

4.   Every power, motivating sin within me; break by fire, in the name of Jesus.

5.   Power of God, root out by fire, unrighteousness in me, in the name of Jesus,

6.   Root of sin in my life; be uprooted by fire, in the name of Jesus.

7.   Every generator of sin in my soul; quench by fire, in the name of Jesus.

## LET EVIL GATES COLLAPSE

1.   Any satanic checkpoint; I pass you by fire, in the name of Jesus.

2. Evil sacrifice in the evil gate against my life; fall down and die, in the name of Jesus.

3. Every incantation in the evil gate to discover my secrets; I blind you by fire, in the name of Jesus.

4. Every evil gate opened by the enemy in my life; I close you forever and ever, in the name of Jesus.

5. I refuse to pay satanic tollgates, in the name of Jesus.

6. My marriage gate, tradition and custom will not open you, in the name of Jesus.

7. Any evil demand that will open the gate to Satan into my life; I reject you, in the name of Jesus.

8. Frustration, I am dead to Christ; so leave me alone, in the name of Jesus.

9. Sin, I will not commit you; I am married to Jesus, in the name of Jesus.

10. Evil gates in my life; I am waiting for you to collapse by force, in the name of Jesus.

11. My tongue, hold your peace; allow God to talk, in the name of Jesus.

12.    Any security demon at the checkpoint; die before I come, in the name of Jesus.

13.    Any evil door opened by worldliness in my life; I close you by fire, in the name of Jesus.

14.    Every spirit of worldliness in my life, what are you waiting for? Die by fire, in the name of Jesus

15.    Any invitation given to worldliness in my life, I withdraw you now, in the name of Jesus.

16.    Any evil passion in my life, what are you waiting for? Disappear, in the name of Jesus.

17.    My desires and affections locked up in the world; jump out by force, in the name of Jesus.

18.    Worldly music and films that have taken over my life; release me by force in the name of Jesus.

19.    Any power engaging me in evil conversation, dressing and worldly enjoyment; release me and die, in the name of Jesus.

20.    Every evil ambition in my life; disappear and leave me alone, in the name of Jesus.

# CHAPTER 5

# EVIL GATES OPEN AND CLOSED

Ahab and his wife, Jezebel, conspired and killed Naboth, the Jezreelite, because of his parcel of land. The Lord confronted Ahab through Elijah, the Tishbite. By killing Naboth and shedding innocent blood, an evil gate was opened to Ahab and his family. The Lord told him that He would bring evil upon him and would take away Ahab's posterity, and would cut off from his house "he that pisseth against the wall, and he that is shut up and left in Israe1." The Lord also said that he would make Ahab's house like the house of Jeroboam, the son of Nebat; and like the house of Baasha, for the provocation wherewith he (Ahab) had provoked Him (God) to anger, and made Israel sin. (1 Kings 21:16-29)

To Jezebel, God said that dogs would eat her by the wall of Jezerel. In addition, to Ahab's household, the Lord said, "He that dieth of Ahab in the city, the gods shall eat; and he that dieth in the field shall the fowls of the air eat" (1Kings 21:21-27). Whenever and wherever an evil gate is opened, many demons enter and possess the people there. If one repents and starts fighting on the Lord's side, he will overcome those demons. Even when you repent in such a place, family or nation, but you are not able to go into spiritual warfare, you may still suffer not as a sinner but as a sluggard, a lazy person, who has refused to use his weapons against his enemies (James 4:7). Evil gates are opened to the children born and those yet unborn in all generations. The representatives of evil gate are legal representatives for all his people in all generations (Exodus 20:5):

*"Thou shalt not bow down thyself to them, nor serve them: for I the LORD thy God am a jealous God, visiting the iniquity of the fathers upon the children unto the third and fourth generation of them that hate me" (Exodus 20:5).*

From the beginning of the world, God has never punished anybody or sent any person to hell because of sin but because they refused to accept a way of salvation, and ignorance or laziness to engage in spiritual warfare. When God forgives, He does not bear grudges. When you are born again and your life destroys the tradition and theology of the religion and customs of the people, handed over to them by evil spirits at the evil gate, the demons will fight to bring you to "order." Nevertheless, your life, preaching, and physical manifestation or demonstration of God's power will reveal the foolishness of idolatry.

Believers should be battle ready as soon as they are born again, or as soon as they see any evil gate opened in their family or any place they find themselves in. Satan and his demons are usurpers. If he (Satan) resisted God and even requested Jesus Christ to bow down for him i.e. to worship him (Satan), he can say the same thing to a holy man or woman of God. Moreover, if you refuse to obey him, you must be ready for battle. Old things have refused to pass away in the lives of many Christians despite the injunction in the word of God to the contrary. We therefore have to use all our available weapons to fight it out.

Don't just watch Satan take away your benefits and thus deny you your rights and privileges. When judgment was passed against the family of Ahab, an evil gate was opened, only Ahab started fighting. Every other member of his family was "enjoying" sin. Ahab refused to feast with the rest of the members of his family (1 Kings 21:25-29). The Lord spoke to Elijah saying, "Because Ahab humbleth himself before me, I will not bring the evil in his days: but 1 will still bring it in his son's days in Ahab's house." All the sacrifices to appease the gods of our fathers at the evil gates amount to a waste of time when God and His son are not involved. Only true repentance and spiritual warfare can move God to stop the actions of the demons invited to the dining table of evil gates.

Your father may be a good man, a moral man and may have given you some guides to this life. However, his righteousness cannot save you, likewise his religion. You have to go to God on personal grounds and settle every account with Him alone. Do not wait for all your family members because salvation is personal. Ahab truly repented at that time; prayed and fasted, but he was only able to shift the consequence of that sin from his own side. He pushed it to the days of his children. The days of his children were therefore demonized by the sins, which their father committed. Are your days demonized because of the sins your ancestors committed? How free are your days? Is innocent blood shed by your ancestors crying in your days? (1 Kings 21:29).

The demons invited by the evil sins of Ahab and his wife at the gate, took the best position in the lives of the sons of Ahab and were ready to strike immediately Ahab died. They stayed for three years without war, premature death, barrenness, lack, late marriage, crises, etc. In fact, they all enjoyed the best of that nation, thinking that all was well. Every opportunity to repent of their sins was mocked at until Ahab died (1 Kings 22:1-3).

*"And they continued three years without war between Syria and Israel. And it came to pass in the third year, that Jehoshaphat the king of Judah came down to the king of Israel. And the king of Israel said unto his servants, know ye that*

*Ramoth in Gilead is ours, and we be still, and*
*take it not out of the hand of the king of Syria?"*
*(I Kings 22:1-3).*

God does not motivate Land disputes, as we witness today. "Don't join a sinner to fight the king of Syria. The king of Syria and Ahab are both in the same boat (cult) just to shed blood." As young person, do not allow the Obas, Igwes, Emirs, and leaders of your nation to drag you into an unnecessary war. Evil communication corrupts good manners.

*"And the king of Israel said unto his servants,*
*Know ye that Ramoth in Gilead is ours, and we*
*be still, and take it not out of the hand of the king*
*of Syria? ⁴And he said unto Jehoshaphat, Wilt*
*thou go with me to battle to Ramoth–gilead? And*
*Jehoshaphat said to the king of Israel, I am as*
*thou art, my people as thy people, my horses as*
*thy horses" (I Kings 22:3-4).*

In addition, the king of Israel said unto his servants, "Know ye that Ramoth in Gilead is ours, and we still, and take it not out of the hand of the king of Syria?" Moreover, he said unto Jehoshaphat, "Will thou go with me to battle to Ramoth-gilead?" In addition, Jehoshaphat said to the king of Israel, "I am as thou art, my people as thy people, my horses as thy horses.

A word is enough for the wise. After three years of prosperity in evil ways, God waited of Jezebel and her children as well as other Israelites to repent but in vain. Already, all the demons invited by Ahab and his wife through evil gates were under starvation and they could not act unless they killed Ahab prematurely. They could not break God's word concerning Ahab.

> *"Seest thou how Ahab humbleth himself before me? because he humbleth himself before me, I will not bring the evil in his days: but in his son's days will I bring the evil upon his house" (1 Kings 21:29).*

The spirits having occupied the house of Ahab knew that unless Ahab was dead, they would not be able to drink the blood at the hand of human beings in Israel because of God's word. These evil spirits then influenced Ahab to declare an unholy war against Syria. Out of over four hundred prophets in Israel, only one called Micaiah was on the Lord's side. The evil spirits deceived all the others. The evil gate was opened and they told Ahab to go to war against Syria because the Lord was going to deliver the Syrians into his hands.

Micaiah was called and he tried to save Ahab and all Israel but instead of the king listening to him, he put the prophet in prison (1 King 22:17-29). That war claimed the life of Ahab prematurely. This war also claimed the lives of most of his supporters in Israel (1 Kings 22:34-37). Ahab did not maintain the promise of God to him. Repenting today and backsliding tomorrow cannot allow God's promise to be fulfilled in your life. What God wants is total separation from sin. Ahab was once broken hut he did not maintain his brokenness.

Brokenness is totally yielding to God at all times. It is not being broken today and going into idolatry tomorrow. Though Ahab enjoyed himself for three years because of his previous brokenness, his later life was sinful; hence, he died a shameful death.

*"So the king died, and was brought to Samaria; and they buried the king in Samaria. And* one

*washed the chariot in the pool of Samaria; and*
*the dogs licked up his blood; and they washed his*
*armor; according unto the word of the LORD*
*which he spake" (I Kings 22:37-38).*

Therefore, the king died and was brought to Samaria.
They buried the king in Samaria. In addition, one washed
the chariot in the pool of Samaria; and the dogs licked up
his blood. They washed his armor, according to the word
of the LORD, which Elijah spake.

## EFFECTS OF EVIL GATES IN AHAB'S FAMILY

The problem with Ahab was that he only closed the evil
gate a little. Moreover, from time to time, he opened it
with sin. Immediately after his death, his wife Jezebel and
her sons, together with other Israelites opened the evil gate
wider with her atrocities. God raised and anointed a man
called Jehu; a young army officer, the son of Jehoshaphat,
the son of Nimshi, to Judge Ahab's family (2 Kings 9:30-
37).

Jezebel was the first victim. Nobody can escape God's judgment. The woman that controlled the whole of Israel and their kings for many years was eventually judged. The woman that chased Prophet Elijah out of the country was eventually judged. A high-ranking witch, who bewitched a whole nation for many years, was judged just in a moment. I am afraid you are going to be judged if you fail to repent. He was the first woman that introduced "make-up" in the Bible. She was and is still the mother of all the women to whom "make-up" is their god (Jeremiah 4:30).

She died but was not accorded burial rites, as she was thrown down from her storied apartment. Her blood was sprinkled on the wall, and dogs later ate her up. Dogs, in a place known as Jezreel, consumed her blood and flesh. People found the great prostitute's skull, feet, and the palms of her hands dismembered, so that nobody could say: "This is Jezebel," according to the word of God as spoken by Elijah.

The eater of flesh and drinker of blood were abandoned for perfect destruction (2Kings 10:1, 6-8, 10-11). The same day was the seal of protection over Ahab's sons removed because they refused to repent. They inherited evil from their father's gate. They were all killed in one day. Ahab opened an evil gate, closed it, and opened it again for his destruction, that of his family, and even the nation, Israel. Sin darkens understanding. Sin is a domineering tyrant. It is a hereditary evil.

Sin is an inward enemy (which is) ready to destroy at the slightest opportunity. It is not to be joked with at all. The problem is that sin is first inherited before it is committed. However, we can overcome sin through the second Adam - the Lord Jesus Christ.

> *"The next day John seeth Jesus coming unto him, and saith, Behold the Lamb of God, which taketh away the sin of the world" (John 1:29).*

Sin dealt with David but he eventually overcame it and fulfilled his destiny (Acts 13:36). He was able to achieve that through his determination.

## DELIVERANCE FROM EVIL ALTARS

Abel took a good decision and God (Genesis 4:4) respected his sacrifice. That is a jump from evil altars. Enoch took a good decision and he walked with God (Genesis 5:18-24). That is another jump from an evil altar.

The Hebrew midwives took a good decision and refused to kill innocent children as directed by Pharaoh. They feared God and disregarded the word of Pharaoh (Exodus 1:15-22). Aaron took a good decision when he offered sacrifices unto the Lord as commanded by Moses. In addition, in confirmation of divine acceptance, "fire came down from heaven and consumed upon the altar the burnt offering and the fat..." (Leviticus 9:6-24).

Phinehas took the best decision when he pursued, overtook, and killed Zimri and Cozbi to avert judgment in Israel (Numbers 25:7-18). Moses took a good decision when though he knew he was to die having been forbidden from going to the Promised Land, he still went ahead and gave the children of Israel good pieces of advice on how to dwell safely in the Promised Land (Deuteronomy 4:21-40; 5:1-33; 21:18-21; 31:1-30; 32:1-52). He also blessed them tribe after tribe and removed the curses placed upon them by their ancestors (Deuteronomy 33:1-29; 34:9-12).

Rahab, the prostitute, took a good decision when she repented and joined the people of God (Joshua 2:1-24). That is also another jump from an evil altar.

Gideon took a good decision when he asked God a good question. He sought to know why evil things were befalling them if God was still with them. He recounted God's goodness to Israel and wanted to know the reason why they were no more being helped by God. He destroyed the altar of Baal (Judges 6:12-32).

Ruth, though a stranger, took a better decision than Orpah, and manifested strong hatred to the gods of the fathers while loving the God of Israel (Ruth 1:14-19, 22). Hannah took a good decision when she decided to leave the congregation of barren women, went to the temple, fought her battle, and defeated the spirit of barrenness (1 Samuel 1:5-6, 9-28). David's mighty men fought on the side of David; a man chosen by God (1 Samuel 22:1-2; 23:8-39). This is another example of a good decision. It is a jump from an evil group to holy company.

A young man, a true prophet of God, boldly went to Bethel and challenged the evil altar that had captured many souls (1 King 13:1-5). You can rebel against your family idol. The four lepers (in Israel) took a good decision when they by their reports, brought deliverance to the people of Israel (2 Kings 7:3-20). This is a move from famine to abundance. The fathers of Aijalon took a good decision when they bought and drove away the inhabitants of Gath (1 Chronicles 8:13).

Manasseh took a good step when he besought the Lord his God, and humbled himself greatly before the God of his father's (2 Chronicles 33:11-16). Isaiah took a good step by responding to God's commandment. He confronted the children of Judah in the days of King Uzziah, Jotham, Ahaz and Hezekiah to repent and turn to their God (Isaiah 1:1-24). Baruch took a good step to publish Jeremiah's words, which had a promise for him (Jeremiah 45:1-5).

Ezekiel also took a good step when he told the people of God's determination to punish sinners who rejected God (Ezekiel 39:1-29). The Ninevites took a good decision after hearing the preaching of Jonah. They believed God, proclaimed a fast and put on sackcloth - from the greatest of them to the least (Jonah 3:1-10).

Joel took a good step when he boldly encouraged the Israelites' with God's promises. He prophesied the pouring of God's spittoon on all flesh (Joel 2:21-32). Amos took a good decision also. He was faithful to divine call, even at Bethel (Amos 7:10-17). Hosea was the prophet of God who took it as his duty to call on and plead with Judah to return to the Lord (Hosea 6:1-3).

By faith and good decision, Micah prophesied about the restoration before the whole of Israel (Micah 4:1-3).

Through faith and good decision, Nahum preached God's goodness and punishment to the rebellions people who refused to repent (Nahum 1:7-15).

By faith and good decision also, Zephaniah advised the Israelites to wait for the Lord's visitation (Zephaniah 3:8-20). By obedience to the word of God and good decision, Habakkuk received a wonderful vision for sinners (Habakkuk 2:1-4, 20).

Daniel took a good decision when he purposed in his heart not to defile himself with the wine and the King's meat (food), and the cup with which the king drank (Daniel 1:8). Obadiah took a good decision when he confronted and prophesied doom to Edom for hating his brother, Jacob (Obadiah 1:8-21). Haggai took a good step when he motivated the people of God to build God's temple (Haggai 11:1-11, 13-15). Malachi was the prophet who stood with God and took a firm decision for tithes and offerings. He declared to his people, the blessings of obedience (Malachi 3:8-18).

Ezra took a good decision, and prepared his heart to seek God in the midst of rebels, who refused to seek God and obey His Jaws (Ezra 7:10). Esther took a good and radical decision to pray and fast in order to save the people of

God. She was the woman who made the popular statement, "If I perish, I perish," in the Bible (Esther 4:10-17).

The children of Israel took a good and positive step when they separated themselves from strangers, confessed their sins, studied God's word, worshipped and blessed the Lord, made a sure covenant with God, and declared God's goodness to themselves (Nehemiah 9:1).

David took a good decision when he decided not to give sleep to his eyes or slumber to his eyelids until he had found a place for the Lord; a habitation for the Almighty God of Jacob (Psalms 132:1-18). The fool in Proverb 17:28, took a good step when he decided not to worry but to hold his peace. The violent took a good step when he decided to take God's kingdom by force (Mathew 11:10-13).

Jairus took a good decision when he despised the shame, humbled himself, identified with Jesus, and besought Him to heal his daughter (Mark 5:22-24, 35-43). Zecharias and his wife, Elizabeth, took a good decision to remain righteous before God, even with their problems, truly believing God (Luke 1:5-17).

Nicodemus, with all his fame and high position took a good decision by not considering his "knowledge without Christ;" throwing away his honor, and going to Christ in the night (John 3:1-3). Julius took a good decision when he courteously entreated Paul and gave him liberty to go to his friends and refresh himself (Acts 28:16, 29-31).

Phoebe, as one of the pillars of the early church, took a good decision to be a source of succor to many, even to Paul (Romans 16:1-2). The people of Macedonia, though poor and under great trials and affliction, took a good decision to give, and they even gave themselves first to Paul and to God (2 Corinthians 8:1-15).

Your decision is very important if you are going to move forward and go to where God wants you to be. The children of Israel moved out from the bondage of Egypt to where God wanted them to be. You can do the same thing. Do not remain where your ancestors kept you. Evil gates are satanic prison yards. Therefore, move beyond satanic limitations and possess your possessions.

# PRAYER POINTS

## DISENGAGING FROM EVIL ALTARS

1. Any power pursuing my life from evil altars; go back to your sender, in the name of Jesus

2. Any demon released from evil altars against my life; be blinded unto death, in the name of Jesus.

3. Every judgement passed against me from the evil altars; expire by force, in the name of Jesus.

4. Every evil door my ancestors have opened on evil altars; be closed by force, in the name of Jesus.

5. I refuse to be imprisoned by the evil altars, in the name of Jesus.

6. I withdraw my life and every evil sacrifice on evil altars, in the name of Jesus.

7. Any evil altar established on my behalf in the waters; be uprooted by thunder, in the name of Jesus.

8. Every promise made by my ancestors in the evil altars; expire by the blood of Jesus, in the name of Jesus.

9.      Any power fighting to retain his ground in my life, I am born again; die by fire, in the name of Jesus.

10.     Demons from evil altars, listen to me; old things are passed away; carry your evil load by fire now, in the name of Jesus.

11.     Blood of Jesus, visit every evil altar working against me by fire, in the name of Jesus.

12.     Any evil inheritance from the evil altars; I reject you with perfection, in the name of Jesus.

13.     I separate the totality of my life from the evil altars, in the name of Jesus.

14.     Every curse of impossibility issued against me from the evil altars; be destroyed, in the name of Jesus.

15.     Any problem flowing into my life from the evil altars; dry up by fire, in the name of Jesus.

16.     Blood of Jesus, separate me from the sins of my ancestors, in the name of Jesus.

17.     I release my destiny from any inherited bondage, in the name of Jesus.

18.     I release myself from every evil domination and control of evil altars, in the name of Jesus.

19. I break and loose myself from every form of demonic bewitchment from evil altars, in the name of Jesus.

20. You evil foundation plantation attacking me from evil altars; come out of my life with all your roots, in the name of Jesus.

21. Lord Jesus, walk back into every second of my life and deliver me from the bondage of evil altars, in the name of Jesus.

22. I withdraw and cancel my name from the register of evil altars, the name of Jesus.

23. I withdraw my pictures, image, and inner-man from evil altars, in name of Jesus.

24. Any power circulating my name in the evil altars for evil purposes; be disgraced, in the name of Jesus.

25. Fire of God, toast every evil material deposited against my life in any evil altar, in the name of Jesus.

26. Let all my adversaries make mistakes on their evil altars that will advance my cause, in the name of Jesus.

27.  I send confusion into the evil altar, and command their plans against me to backfire, in the name of Jesus.

28.  I remove my name from the book of failure in the evil altars, in the name of Jesus.

29.  Darkness; posses every evil altar attacking my destiny, in the name of Jesus.

30.  You my parental covenant and curses working against me in the evil altar; break and release me, in the name of Jesus.

31.  I jump out from every satanic trap set against me on any evil altar, in the name of Jesus.

32.  Evil spirit from any evil altar; my life is a no-go area, in the name of Jesus.

33.  Every inherited curse from the evil altars, break and release me, in the name of Jesus.

34.  All the doors of blessings closed by the evil altars; open by fire, in the name of Jesus.

35.  I dismantle every hindrance, obstacle or blockage put in my way from the evil altars, in the name of Jesus.

36.  Any conscious and unconscious oath from the evil altar working against my life; break, in the name of Jesus.

37.  Every evil mark, incision, and writing placed upon my spirit, body and soul from the evil altar; be wiped off by the blood of Jesus, in the name of Jesus.

38.  Any evil foundation rebuilt by the enemy against my life; be demolished, in the name of Jesus.

39.  Any evil bird attacking my life from evil altars; die without mercy, in the name of Jesus.

40.  Any evil attempt to return me to my ancestral curses and covenant; be resisted by fire, in the name of Jesus.

41.  Any demon attached to my life from evil altars; be bound forever and ever, in the name of Jesus.

42.  Any covenant binding me to the problem from the evil altars; break by fire, in the name of Jesus.

43.  Wall of the fire of the Holy Ghost; compass me forever against demonic attacks from the evil altars, in the name of Jesus.

44. I release myself from the grip of any problem from the evil altars, in the name of Jesus.

45. Blood of Jesus, cleanse every organ of my body from the evil altars, in the name of Jesus.

46. Any problem transferred into my life from the evil altars; die forever and ever, in the name of Jesus.

47. Blood of Jesus, flush out of my system any inherited problem from any evil altar, in the name of Jesus.

48. Oh hands of God; arrest any satanic soldier firing against me from any evil altar, in the name of Jesus.

49. Let the rod of the wicked rising against my destiny from my family altar be rendered impotent for my sake, in the name of Jesus.

50. I bind all evil spirits in me and the ones attacking me from any evil altar, in the name of Jesus.

51. Every evil spirit trying to rob me of the will of God for my life; fall down and die, in the name of Jesus.

52. I tear down any evil altar that has vowed to destroy my life, in the name of Jesus

53.    I tear down the stronghold of Satan attacking me from evil altars, in the name of Jesus.

54.    I smash every plan of the enemy formed against me in the evil altars, in the name of Jesus.

55.    Every witchcraft attack targeted against me from any evil altar; backfire, in the name of Jesus.

56.    All stubborn spirits pursuing me from the evil altars; pursue yourselves into death, in the name of Jesus.

57.    Any power standing against my prayer life in any evil altar; die forever and ever, in the name of Jesus.

58.    I renounce and revoke any signing of my name over Satan, in the name of Jesus.

59.    Every legal ground that guardian/ancestral spirits have in my life; be destroyed by the blood of Jesus, in the name of Jesus.

60.    Every ancestral evil altar prospering against me; be dashed to pieces on the wall of fire, in the name of Jesus.

61.   Every legal ground that ancestral guardian spirits have in my destiny; be destroyed by fire, in the name of Jesus.

62.   Every grip of the evil relationship of the ancestral worship of my ancestors over my life; break and release me, in the name of Jesus.

63.   Every covenant with water spirits from the evil altars; break and release me, in the name of Jesus.

64.   Every ancestral embargo from the evil altar; be lifted by fire by force, in the name of Jesus.

65.   Every good thing stolen by ancestral embargo from the evil altar; be lifted by fire by force, in the name of Jesus.

66.   Every good thing stolen by ancestral demons from my ancestors, I recover you now, in the name of Jesus.

67.   Every ancestral chain tying me to any evil altar; break and release me, in the name of Jesus.

68.   Every ancestral evil life pattern dominating my life; release me and die, in the name of Jesus.

69. Any power from the evil altar keeping backs my blessings because of ancestral vows; release it by force, in the name of Jesus.

70. Any evil sacrifice to evil altars by my ancestors fighting against my destiny; I challenge you by the blood of Jesus.

71. Every vow and decision made against me in any, altar contrary to the will of God; lose your hold by fire, in the name of Jesus.

72. I withdraw anything representing me on every evil altar, in the name of Jesus.

73. Oh Lord, send the blood of Jesus to destroy anything fashioned against me in any evil altar, in the name of Jesus.

74. Thunder of God; strike any evil priest that has vowed to destroy me on the evil altars, in the name of Jesus.

75. Every satanic priest ministering against me at the evil altars; receive madness now, in the name of Jesus.

76. Sword of fire; fight against my enemies at the evil altars, in the name of Jesus.

77. Any hand that is ready to retaliate against me in any evil altar; break in the name of Jesus.

78. Every evil altar at my village that has arrested my destiny; release it now by force, in the name of Jesus.

79. Any evil hand holding my prosperity; wither, in the name of Jesus.

80. Stubborn evil priest ready to strike at my family; drink your own blood and eat your flesh, in the name of Jesus.

# CHAPTER 6

# MIGHTY WEAPONS IN THE HANDS OF SLUGGARDS

*"How long wilt thou sleep, O sluggard? When wilt thou arise out of thy sleep? Yet a little sleep, a little slumber, a little folding of the hands to sleep: So shall thy poverty come as one that travelleth, and thy want as an armed man"* (Proverbs 6:9-11).

### Gehazi (2 Kings 5:20-27)

The sin of Gehazi was very bad but not the worst sin ever committed. Truly, he committed iniquity but God was waiting for him to repent and say: "Lord, I am sorry. Please forgive me." Instead of repentance, Gehazi chose to tell lies. Gehazi had seen his master and his God pardon greater sins than his. He had seen and heard about God's great mercy and goodness. He knew God as the Lord God of Abraham, Isaac and Jacob. He knew God as Elohim (the Strong One). He knew him also as Adonai (Master or Lord). These names imply rulership over His creation. Gehazi knew that God had absolute dominion and that in Him is the ability to do all things; yet he died a leper.

When Ahab sinned and humbled himself, the Lord God forgave him. Nevertheless, when Gehazi sinned in the house of God under the leadership of a beloved prophet with a double portion anointing, he simply said amen to the curse placed upon him (2 Kings 5:26-27). Gehazi, instead of using the weapons of humility, true repentance, etc., proudly left the greatest man of his generation. A stranger came and received his healing from leprosy but Gehazi, a member of the commonwealth of Israel, became and remained a leper throughout his life. What a shame that a foundation member of a living church will usher people into the house of God to receive from the Lord while he or she dies with his or her own problems. What a great disappointment that testimonies have departed from old members of the church (2 Kings 5:13-14).

Gehazi should have wept before Elisha and confessed his sin. Ananias should have confessed to Peter. Though Sapphira agreed with her husband earlier, she should have repented. However, she decided to meet her husband in hell fire. What are you waiting for? Would you like to dislike your fathers? Do not be careless with your soul. Repent of your sins and the Lord will heal you and deliver you. Gehazi took the cases of many people who were in bondage to his master, Elisha, but when he was placed under bondage, he could not pray to free himself (2 Kings 4:12-17).

Many believers today are giving the testimonies of what God is doing in their churches and in the lives of other people. They are in charge of testimonies in their Christian group but they themselves have no testimonies. Some people answer "Blessing" (as their name) but the blessings of God are still very far from them. Some answer "Grace" but they do not have enough grace for a single miracle.

God forbid that I will answer "Miracle" as a name without a single miracle in my life. Now, I want you to say that it is now your turn to give testimony (2 Kings 8:4-6). The curse placed on Gehazi was forever and ever but we have a God who can heal and the healing remains forever (2 Kings 5:27). If you see an Israelite today with leprosy, he or she must have come from the seed of Gehazi. That is what we call an evil gate or evil inheritance.

It may be true that you know God but you may not know Him as Jehovah Rapha, meaning, the Lord that healeth us (Exodus 15:26). You are supposed to know Him as Jehovah Jireh, which means (that) the Lord will provide (Genesis 22:13-14).

The blood of Abner was to cry against Israel forever but David intervened and limited it to a particular family in Israel (2 Samuel 3:28-29). Joab or any other person in that family was free to take up the challenge and silence the blood. An individual in that family could also come out and separate himself and his family from the crying blood of Abner. Joab had all the weapons to silence the blood of Abner but he did not.

Cain had all the opportunity to become a great man like Abel but he did not use it. Rather, he fought his brother and even God with all his strength (Genesis 4:3-10). God took (some) time to tell Cain the reason he was not in prosperity, yet he (Cain) failed to pay attention.

We have a very thin line between success and failure. The decision you take in this life matters a lot. The first captain with his fifty soldiers in 2 Kings 1:9-10, failed because he had no respect or regard for the man of God, Elijah. Your manner of approach to persons and God can build or destroy you. The captain addressed the prophet (Elijah) thus: "Thou man of God, the king hath said, come down." The second captain said to Elijah: "O man of God, thus hath the king said, comedown quickly." The third captain of fifty went and fell on his knees before Elijah and pleaded with him; "O man of God, I pray thee, let my life, and the lives of these unfaithful servants be precious in thy sight..." No matter your position, God is God and his standard is unchangeable.

**Reuben** (Genesis 49:1-4).

*"And Jacob called unto his sons, and said,*
*Gather yourselves together, that I may tell you*
*that which shall befall you in the last*
*days. Gather yourselves together, and hear, ye*

*sons of Jacob; and hearken unto Israel your father... Reuben, thou art my firstborn, my might, and the beginning of my strength, the excellency of dignity, and the excellency of power: Unstable as water, thou shalt not excel; because thou wentest up to thy father's bed; then defiledst thou it: he went up to my couch" (Genesis 49:1-4).*

The last words of a man before he dies are highly esteemed. Wise people in all generations pay close attention to people's last words. Jacob, probably with a good mind, called his children together to bless them. Nevertheless, Reuben being the eldest, who was supposed to bring his younger ones together, was not ready to cooperate with his aged father.

The last words of a man, whether a sinner or a saint, are backed up with some powers - negative or positive - depending on whom the person served. Unfortunately, many careless Christians (like Reuben) are not ready to hearken unto Israel their father.

When Jacob started talking to Reuben, it was like praise but in the middle of his (Jacob's) speech to Reuben, he remembered all the offences of this young man - all his unprofitable arguments with his son Reuben, and also

Reuben's immoral life. All his unrighteousness, - fornication, wickedness, covetousness, malice, envy against his brother Joseph, deceit, whispering, backbiting, disobedience to his parents, etc.

Jacob had wished to see Reuben repent and confess before his death, but to no avail. The greatest disappointment of a man is to see any of his children unrepentant on the day of his death. At the time of Jacob's death, his first son, Reuben, was still unrepentant concerning his evil ways. What a shame and disappointment for such a man to observe that all his counsel, home training etc., which he dished out to his child was rejected even unto his death.

Reuben's life was filled with confusion. Reuben was the unstable water of the Old Testament (Genesis 49:4; James 1:8). This was a man that Jacob tried to trust but all his efforts failed. Reuben was a man given to change - "unstable as water." Immorality is a dangerous sin; it is very destructive. One of the many seeds of immorality is an unstable spirit, the spirit of a chameleon or an unreliable spirit.

The major problem of man in all generations is disobedience to parents (Ephesians 6:1-3). Cain was destroyed because of disobedience. The sons of Noah ended (their lives) in shame because of disobedience to their parents. Zimri and Cozbi died because of disobedience to their parents. The sons of Eli also died because of disobedience to their parents (1 Samuel 12:12-17). Samson also died because of disobedience to his parents.

The very day Jacob said to his first son, Reuben, "Thou shall not excel" was the day Reuben's problems started; although he (Reuben) was married and had many promising children, a good house in Egypt, the right of first son (birthright), etc. After his father's statement, he probably might have laughed it off, but an evil seed was sown in his family forever.

In the Book of Numbers, chapter one; when Moses numbered the children of Israel tribe by tribe, though Reuben married early and got children before many of his brothers, the tribe of Reuben had only forty sixty thousand, five hundred soldiers while the blessed tribe of Judah had seventy four thousand, six hundred soldiers. The tribe of Dan had sixty-two thousand, seven hundred soldiers (Numbers 1:20-21, 27, 39). Between the Book of Genesis 49 and Numbers, the curse placed upon the tribe of Reuben was very much in operation (Numbers 2:10-11).

In Numbers 16, Dathan and Abiram, the sons of Eliab, and On, the son of Peleth, son of Reuben, took men and rose against Moses and God (Numbers 16:1-2). The Book of Jude 4 says that they were ungodly men, turning the grace of our God into lasciviousness, and denying the only Lord God, and our Lord Jesus Christ."

When their father Reuben was cursed, he did not use the weapon of repentance, prayer of confession, and fasting. From this tribe, men always rose against God and His chosen men (Jude 4, 8 and 16). When any family is under a curse, members of that family will always die prematurely (Numbers 16:12, 25-27, 32-34).

By the time Moses was rounding off his ministry (like Jacob), he called Israel together, and this time the tribe of Reuben was almost extinct as a result of the curse placed on it by Jacob, the father of Reuben.

In Deuteronomy 33:6, Moses, under high divine anointing, broke the curse. Nevertheless, before this time, premature death was so rampant in the tribe of Reuben, especially against the men in every quarter of that tribe. There were more widows than widowers.

The young men who died were those who went to war, but never came back alive. Most of the bad things that happened in Israel came from this and other cursed tribes. Satan used them to test all new evil introduced in the nation. In addition, any other tribe or person who cooperated with them was affected. When you enter into a marriage partnership with a cursed person or family, you become cursed. When you go into a business partnership with a cursed person, you will be affected too. Anybody who wants and determines to help a cursed person must be holy and very prayerful; otherwise, the person will also go into captivity with the cursed one (1 Chronicles 5:1-10, 25-26). Victory can only come to a cursed person through repentance and warfare prayers (1 Chronicles 5:18-20).

## Men Under Pain

*"And the fifth angel poured out his vial upon the seat of the beast; and his kingdom was full of darkness; and they gnawed their tongues for pain, blasphemed the God of heaven because of their pains and their sores, and repented not of their deeds... And there fell upon men a great hail out of heaven,* every stone *about the weight of a talent: and men blasphemed God because of*

*the plague of the hail; for the plague thereof was*
*exceeding great" (Revelation 16:10-11, 21).*


The source of pain, affliction and sickness is Satan. Though the causes are many, the main cause is sin. Many names given to Satan in the scriptures show his evil works. Satan is called a sinner in the book of 1 John 3:8. He is the father of all sinners and liars (John 8:44). He is also referred to in the Bible as the ruler of darkness (Ephesians 6:12).

In fact, every evil work and almost every pain is associated with Satan. Evil spirits also assist Satan in his attacks against man. These evil spirits are very destructive. They can attack people with all manner of problems like spiritual and physical blindness, deafness, lunacy and mania. At times, God sends his punishment to the world when humankind insists on rebellion against God. That was the case with the Egyptians when they insisted on destroying God's covenant people - the Israelites.

Likewise, in Revelation 16:10-11, and 21, the fullness of God's wrath will be released upon a world of rebellious people. Grievous sores will be unleashed upon men and women that will take the mark of the beast or those who are worshiping (or will worship) the image of the beast. In verse 2, instead of repentance, the suffering sinners blasphemed the God of heaven because of their pain and sores.

Suffering and painful situations can draw men closer to God, make them change their church, pass through deliverance, and become recognized members of a deliverance ministry. Nevertheless, once they have not repented, confessed and forsaken their evil ways (sins), they are still deceiving themselves (Isaiah 55:6-7).

## All Flesh

*"In the six hundredth year of Noah's life, in the second month, the seventeenth day of the month, the same day were all the fountains of the great deep broken up, and the windows of heaven were opened. And the rain was upon the earth forty days and forty nights... And all flesh died that moved upon the earth, both of fowl, and of cattle, and of beast, and of every creeping thing that creepeth upon the earth, and every man: All in whose nostrils* was *the breath of life, of all that*

was *in the dry* land, *died. And every living substance was destroyed which was upon the face of the ground, both man, and cattle, and the creeping things, and the fowl of the heaven; and they were destroyed from the earth: and Noah only remained* alive, *and they that* were *with him in the ark. And the waters prevailed upon the earth an hundred and fifty days"* (<u>Genesis 7:11-12, 21-24</u>).

These people must have tried all means to escape death. They must have schemed and used human wisdom to no avail. Some might have climbed their storey buildings, entered underground buildings, etc. Engineers and builders of those days must have tried to save those men of their generation. Presidents, skilful men and women; men full of knowledge and understanding must have tried in vain to save their generation. The witches and wizards, magicians, astrologers and the sorcerer's of that generation must have tried in vain to deliver themselves. Nevertheless, they all perished. They must have cried, prayed, fasted compulsorily but all was in vain.

Some people must have regretted and repented but it was very late (Isaiah 55:6-7). They sought the Lord, but it was too late for them. They must have called upon God but it was all in vain. The word of God says: "Seek ye the Lord while He may be found; call ye upon Him while He is near" (Isaiah 55:6). Almost every human being prays today, especially in the Pentecostal circle. Only few of them pray at the right time. Many of the few who pray at the right time pray wrong prayers. Some pray at the wrong places, where God cannot hear them (verse 7).

There is a demand from God to every sinner before prayers can be answered. Something has to be forsaken. There is a way that has to be forsaken. There is a returning that should be accomplished. There is a thought that should be fought with your full strength before pardon will come from God.

You cannot insist on your evil ways, receive full pardon, and complete deliverance. The true mercy of God cannot come until you fully return unto God, your Almighty Creator. On the day of God's wrath against all flesh, according to the scriptures, all fountains of the great deep broke up and the windows of heaven were opened. They (fountains) opened not to bless men but to destroy them.

In addition, it rained upon this earth forty days and nights against men.

Men tried their best to help themselves but their best failed them. Every human effort failed, and all flesh died. In fact, every living man and animal was destroyed in the flood. The waters remained upon the earth for one hundred and fifty days to make sure that every man died. Moreover, all the men and animals in the world then, except those in the Ark, died; all were destroyed by the flood.

# PRAYER POINTS

## WEAPONS AGAINST EVIL ALTARS

1. Any fear attacking my life from any evil altar, receive the fire of God and burn to ashes, in the name of Jesus.

2. Any power assigned to destroy me from the evil altars; destroy yourself, in the name of Jesus.

3. Any power assigned to drink my blood and eat my flesh from the evil altars, eat your own flesh and drink your own blood, in the name of Jesus.

4. Any power in charge of the problems in my life; kill yourself on the evil altars, in the name of Jesus.

5. Holy Ghost, arise in your power and deliver me by fire from any evil altar, in the name of Jesus.

6. Every spiritual thief from the evil altars sent against me; die, in the name of Jesus.

7. I arrest every demon anointed to destroy my destiny on any evil altar, in the name of Jesus.

8. Oh Lord, send your angels to bring back every good thing stolen from me at the evil altars, in the name of Jesus.

9.    Every spiritual evil caterer from the evil altars; be fed on your own blood, in the name of Jesus.

10.   Every cauldron of witchcraft caging my life in the evil altars; be scattered by fire, in the name of Jesus.

11.   Divine whirlwind, scatter any evil altar against my life, in the name of Jesus.

12.   Wind of fire, locate the evil altars holding my life in bondage and destroy them, in the name of Jesus.

13.   Every masquerade attacking me from the evil altar; be unmasked by fire, in the name of Jesus.

14.   I hold the blood of Jesus against snails and tortoises anointing, and other things working against me from evil altars, in the name of Jesus.

15.   I plead the blood of Jesus upon any evil altar against my life, in the name of Jesus.

16.   I sprinkle the blood of Jesus on all evil altars, in the name of Jesus.

17.   I spread unquenchable fire upon all evil altar worldwide, in the name of Jesus.

18. Blood of Jesus; speak destruction against the evil altars ministering failure in my life, in the name of Jesus.

19. I apply the blood of Jesus over the evil altars working against me, in the name of Jesus.

20. I draw a circle of fire and the blood of Jesus around my family's evil altar, in the name of Jesus.

21. I overcome you Satan by the blood of Jesus on all evil altars, in the name of Jesus.

22. Evil altars of sickness; I am redeemed by the blood of Jesus; die, in the name of Jesus.

23. Blood of Jesus, speak confusion against evil priests working against me on the evil altars, in the name of Jesus.

24. Blood of Jesus, speak destruction into every evil altar and its priests ministering against my life, in the name of Jesus.

25. Blood of Jesus; Holy Ghost fire; dry up every evil tree standing against me, in the name of Jesus.

26. I minister death into any evil altar against my life, in the name of Jesus.

27. I enter into the Holy of Holies by the blood of Jesus, and I destroy every evil altar, in the name of Jesus.

28. Oh hand of God; pull down any evil altar erected for my sake, in the name of Jesus.

29. I hold the blood of Jesus against any evil power, attacking me from the evil altars, in the name of Jesus.

30. Blood of Jesus; attack my attackers of goodness from the evil altars, in the name of Jesus.

31. Blood of Jesus, recover my loosed and imprisoned blessings on the evil altars, in the name of Jesus.

32. My foreign benefit; the blood of Jesus is calling you; escape from the evil altars, in the name of Jesus.

33. Satanic banks in the evil altars; release my finances by fire, in the name of Jesus.

# CHAPTER 7

# THE ARK OF SALVATION

The ark of Noah is compared to the city of refuge (in the Bible) and a call to salvation through Jesus Christ. In the days of Noah, God called the world to salvation. He is still extending the same call to everybody in the world today. Very soon the trumpet will sound:

"For the Lord Himself shall descend from heaven with a shout, with the voice of the archangel, and with the trump of God: and the dead in Christ shall rise first. Then we which are alive and remain shall be caught up together with them in the clouds, to meet the Lord in the air" (like Noah who was lifted up above others in his generation) (1 Thess. 4:16). As Noah escaped death among his generation, so shall those who receive Christ and live according to God's standard escape the soon coming judgement of destruction (Revelation 20:12-15, 21:8; 22:14-15).

## PAIN IN SODOM AND GOMORRAH

*"The sun was risen upon the earth when Lot entered into Zoar. Then the LORD rained upon Sodom and upon Gomorrah brimstone and fire from the LORD out of heaven; And he overthrew those cities, and all the plain, and all the inhabitants of the cities, and that which grew upon the ground" (Genesis 19:23-25).*

As soon as the sun rose on that particular day, and immediately Lot entered into the city called Zoar, the Lord rained upon Sodom and Gomorrah brimstone and fire (Genesis 19:12-14). Preaching of the word of God is going on everywhere today. Sinners are being warned every minute of the day to repent and believe in Christ in order to escape the impending danger, but it seems to them that these preachers are joking. The brimstone and fire that came upon the inhabitants of Sodom and Gomorrah affected people of all levels - men and women - and nobody could help another.

There was confusion as in Noah's days. The fire of God's judgement visited and destroyed everybody. People must have prayed under such pain and agony but it was too late. Do not wait until it becomes too late for you. Seek the Lord now when you can still find Him; call upon Him while He is near. Forsake your evil ways and follow the way of God.

People with God's knowledge but who refused to repent in that generation must have called on God; mentioning His attributes but to no avail. They might have called Him. The Lord God of Abraham, God of Lot etc, yet no help came. They might have called Him the great God; Ancient of days; Great I am that I am; Jehovah Jireh, Jehovah Shalom (the Lord our peace), Jehovah Shammah (the Lord is present). However, at that particular time, He refused to be present in their pain.

The Lord is infinite but not ready to manifest in the pain of a sinner whose time has expired. Do not allow God's time for you to expire before you begin to seek Him. Seek the Lord while he may be found; call upon Him while He is near (Luke 17:26-32). Do not allow what you will eat or drink to keep you off the ark of salvation. Do not allow marriage or business to prevent you from being raptured. They sold; they planted and built. What are those things that are keeping you out of the ark of salvation? Always remember Lot's wife. "If thy hand offend thee, cut it off, and if thine eye offend thee, pluck it out (Matt. 5:30). It is better to thee to enter the kingdom of God with nothing (like Lazarus the beggar) than to be cast into hell fire "where their worms dieth not and the fire is not quenched"(Mark 9:44).

## MEN UNDER PAIN AT SHECHEM

*"And it came to pass on the third day, when they were sore, that two of the sons of Jacob, Simeon and Levi, Dinah's brethren, took each man his sword, and came upon the city boldly, and slew all the males. And they slew*

*Hamor and Shechem his son with the edge of the sword, and took Dinah out of Shechem's house, and went out"* (Genesis 34:25-26).

On the third day of the circumcision of the men at Shechem, when they were sore; under excruciating pain, Simeon and Levi, two of the sons of Jacob, Dinah's brothers, took their swords and slew all the helpless men of war who were under serious pain. They might have cried, pleaded for mercy and promised Simeon and Levi many things but to no avail. They might have called the name of every god in their nation but that did not appeal to the two brothers.

Are you in pain? Are you sick and afflicted? If you are born again, you do not need to watch problems destroy you. Rise up and fight them. "Is any among you afflicted? Let him pray. Is anyone sick among you? Let him call the elders of the Church. In addition, let them pray over him, anointing him with oil in the name of the Lord. Moreover, the prayer of faith shall have the sick, and the Lord shall raise him up and if he has committed sins they shall be forgiven him (James 5:13).

Are your sins forgiven? If not, "confess your faults one to another and pray one for another that you may be healed. The effectual fervent prayer of a righteous man (after all the above steps) availeth much" (James 5:16).

There are some problems that will not go, and deliverance that will never take place, until confession of sins is made to one another, and until prayers are made for one another. No matter how much you pray, no matter the number of deliverance exercises you undergo, your prayer cannot avail much until certain steps are taken.

You must turn away from all known sins. You must have a change of mind, purpose, and action. You must abhor or hate sin with perfect hatred. Once you repent, the Lord will pardon your sins, and your sins will be blotted out. You must be reconciled to God. There must be restitution, which means restoring everything to its rightful owner. Only then, shall there be joy in heaven and on earth for your salvation. It is only then that you will be able to fight the consequences of sin effectively. Otherwise, you will have partial freedom. Nevertheless, we need total deliverance and preservation from sin, evil, and their consequences. You must fight and be delivered fully from pain, enemies, infirmities, physical powers, and slavery.

*"Beloved, I wish above all things that thou mayest prosper and be in health, even as thy oul prospereth" (3 John 2).*

# DEATH OF ALL THE FIRSTBORNS IN EGYPT

The Lord smote them at midnight, and all the firstborns in Egypt died. They all died; from the firstborn of pharaoh that sat on the throne, unto the firstborn of the captive that was in the dungeon. One of the most painful deaths is the unexpected one. These firstborns must have cried, screamed, and called for help to no avail. The most "painful" of all pains is the one that is coming from the Creator. This is because at that point in time, no man can render any help.

The Book of Proverbs says that those who reject God will be helpless in the day of their trouble:

*"I will also laugh at your calamity; I will mock when your fear cometh. Then shall they shall call upon me, but I will not answer, they shall seek me early, but they shall not find me" (Proverbs 1:26-28)*

That night was a horrible night. All the great men in Egypt were around that midnight: the magicians, all the wise men and the great army of Egypt were there but none could render any help on the day of God's wrath. In fact, they wanted dead bodies and God supplied them (Exodus 1:15-22; Psalm 78:50-51; 105:36; Ezekiel 32:31-32).

# THE HOST OF THE EGYPTIAN ARMY IN PAINS

*"And the children of Israel went into the midst of the sea upon the dry ground: and the waters were a wall unto them on their right hand, and on their left. And the Egyptians pursued, and went in after them to the midst of the sea, even all Pharaoh's horses, his chariots, and his*

*horsemen. And it came to pass, that in the morning watch the LORD looked unto the host of the Egyptians through the pillar of fire and of the cloud, and troubled the host of the Egyptians, And took off their chariot wheels, that they drave them heavily: so that the Egyptians said, Let us flee from the face of Israel; for the LORD fighteth for them against the Egyptians. And the LORD said unto Moses, Stretch out thine hand over the sea, that the waters may come again upon the Egyptians, upon their chariots, and upon their horsemen. And Moses stretched forth his hand over the sea, and the sea returned to his strength when the morning appeared; and the Egyptians fled against it; and the LORD overthrew the Egyptians in the midst of the sea. And the waters returned, and covered the chariots, and the horsemen,* and *all the host of Pharaoh that came into the sea after them; there remained not so much as one of them. But the children of Israel walked upon dry* land *in the midst of the sea; and the waters* were *a wall unto them on their right hand, and on their left. Thus, the LORD saved Israel that day out of the hand*

*of the Egyptians; and Israel saw the Egyptians
dead upon the seashore. And Israel saw that
great work which the LORD did upon the
Egyptians: and the people feared the LORD, and
believed the LORD, and his servant Moses"
(Exodus 14:22-31).*

This was a great pain in the midst of the sea. The horses
and the riders were altogether overthrown in the chambers
of the queen of the coast. The Lord troubled the host of
the Egyptians, took off their chariot wheels, and they were
all destroyed under great pain. What torment! They must
have been in terrible pain. It is a dangerous thing to suffer
without God's help.

## NADAB AND ABIHU

*"And Nadab and Abihu, the sons of Aaron, took
either of them his censer, and put fire therein,
and put incense thereon, and offered strange fire
before the LORD, which he commanded them
not. And there went out fire from the LORD, and
devoured them, and they died before the LORD"
(Leviticus 10:1-2).*

Right inside the temple of God, the two sons of Aaron - Nadab and Abihu - became careless about following the laws of God concerning sacrifices. As a result, God destroyed them with fire. Anybody who continues in his sinful way instead of God's way is negotiating for pain. The pain of Nadab and Abihu came right inside the temple and destroyed them. When their pain started, nobody could help them from the beginning to the end. Though Moses and Aaron were there, they could do nothing.

Once your problem is from God, the only wise step you should take is to repent, confess your sins and forsake them. Going from one place to the other cannot help you. Rather, you have to settle down and ask yourself some questions. Examine yourself in the light of the word of God. Some people pray fire prayers, go for deliverance a number of times, and visit great men of God, but they are not ready to repent.

> *"And he brought me into the inner court of the LORD'S house, and, behold, at the door of the temple of the LORD, between the porch and the altar,* were *about five and twenty men, with their*

*backs toward the temple of the LORD, and their faces toward the east; and they worshipped the sun toward the east... Therefore will I also deal in fury: mine eye shall not spare, neither will I have pity: and though they cry in mine ears with a loud voice,* yet *will I not hear them" (Ezekiel 8:16, 18).*

*"And the son of an Israelitish woman, whose father* was *an Egyptian, went out among the children of Israel: and this son of the Israelitish* woman *and a man of Israel strove together in the camp; And the Israelitish woman's son blasphemed the name* of the LORD, *and cursed. And they brought him unto Moses: (and his mother's name* was *Shelomith, the daughter of Dibri, of the tribe of Dan :) And they put him in ward, that the mind of the LORD might be shewed them. And the LORD spake unto Moses, saying" (Leviticus 24:10-13).*

The pain of this young man started when he was confined in the prison. He was in custody alone without God until the will of God was made clear to the people. Eventually, the Lord said to Moses:

> *"Bring forth him that hath cursed without the camp; and let all that heard him lay their hands upon his head, and let all the congregation stone him" (Leviticus 24:14).*

## PAIN ON KORAH, DATHAN AND ABIRAM

### (Numbers 16:1-3, 31-34).

The earth opened its mouth and swallowed Korah, Dathan, and Abiram and everything that belonged to them; they went down into the grave alive. When the ground split and the earth opened its mouth, they were swallowed together with their households and all their possessions. The earth closed over them and they perished instantly. They cried bitterly and instead of receiving help from people around them, those that should have helped them ran away, fearing that the earth would also swallow them

> *"And all Israel that were round about them fled at the cry of them: for they said, lest the earth*

*swallow us up* also. *And there came out a fire*
*from the LORD, and consumed the two hundred*
*and fifty men that offered incense... Now they*
*that died in the plague were fourteen thousand*
*and seven hundred, beside them that died about*
*the matter of Korah" (Numbers 16:34-35, 49).*

## PAIN FROM IMMORALITY

### (Numbers 31:13-24)

*"Now therefore kill every male among the little*
*ones, and kill every woman that hath known man*
*by lying with him. But all the women children,*
*that have not known a man by lying with him,*
*keep alive for yourselves" (Numbers 31:17-18).*

Sexual immorality brings pain unto death. Any
unconfessed sin brings terrible torment. The devil can
allow you to commit immorality today only to pay for it
tomorrow. The daughters of Moab committed immorality
through the advice of Balaam in Numbers 25, but they
paid with their lives in Numbers 31. It takes some years
for the "seed" of HIV to germinate.

There are certain problems that virgins can never suffer. Some miracles can never take place in the lives of immoral, unrepentant people.

Sihon, King of Heshbon, died in pain (Deuteronomy 2:26-37). This king died along with his sons and his people (Deuteronomy 3:6). He rejected the pleading of the children of Israel. He became stubborn and made his heart obstinate. Sihon and all his soldiers were destroyed at Jahaz (Deuteronomy 2:32-36).

## ACHAN AND HIS FAMILY IN PAIN

### (Joshua 7:22-26).

The tragic story of Achan, who stole the Babylonian garments is a big lesson today. The sin of Achan attracted punishment to him and his family, as well as all that he had. Sin is contagious, and destructive (Exodus 20:5). The whole of Israel stoned Achan and members of his family to death and burnt them with fire. Such is the consequence of sin.

## SISERA DIED UNDER PAIN

### (Judges 4:16-24).

The hosts of Sisera fell by the edge of the sword; and there was not a man left; all died under pain. Somehow, Sisera escaped. He however died when he least expected death. He must have wept and cried for help but none came. In addition, under the greatest pain, he died in the hands of a woman. You may have escaped great battles of your life but you still need to be very careful. After all, Adam and Eve overcame every other big and dangerous animal in the Garden of Eden but the serpent overcame them.

Abel pleased God and God respected his sacrifice but household wickedness destroyed and terminated his destiny. The great sons of God in Genesis 6, failed by marrying anyhow. Although they were once called the sons of God, they later became wicked and their thoughts and imaginations were aimed at doing evil. Therefore, God destroyed them.

Sisera escaped death and ran away to the tent of Jael. Sisera's hosts were all killed; but he (Sisera) escaped only to die in the house of a woman. What a shame! The sons of Noah entered the ark and escaped the destruction of the world in their generation. Nevertheless, they came back to build without divine approval and God therefore scattered them, and confounded their language.

Lot, after escaping the immorality and outright disobedience in Sodom and Gomorrah, fell by committing the worst type of sexual immorality - with his own daughters. Hagar, the obedient house cleaner of Sarah, was elevated to be the wife of the greatest man of her generation. Nevertheless, she turned and despised her mistress and was therefore demoted.

Nadab and Abihu, after being faithful and were ordained to be the priests of the most High God later offered a strange fire before the Most High God, and they were consequently slain right in the pulpit, by the fire of God, in spite of their "holy garment." No matter your title and whatever you have done for God, once you sin against God and refuse to come back to Him in repentance, you will be in trouble.

The mixed multitude, though they came out from Egypt, crossed the Red Sea, and sang with melodious voices. However, immediately they began to gossip and speak against their leader, and remembered the food, enjoyment and pleasures of sin in Egypt, the Lord plagued them. Miriam and Aaron were elder sister and elder brother to Moses respectively. They actually knew where he was born, took care of him, saw his nakedness and all his human weaknesses. Nevertheless, once they spoke against him; not respecting the anointing of God on him (Moses), Miriam became leper.

Though Moses had fought and won many battles, the day he smote the Rock twice instead of speaking to it, the Lord said:

"Ye shall not bring this congregation into the land which I have given them…" (Deuteronomy 4:21-26).

Though Saul, the first king of Israel, was ordained king by God, fought the Lord's battles and won many times, the day he began to undertake sacrifices, which was the due of the priests, his kingship was taken from him. Though he was still on the throne for many more years, the Lord had stopped speaking to him. You may still be occupying a respected office but the Lord may have stopped speaking to you long ago, (1Chronicles 18:1-14, 1 Samuel 18:20, 27-28, 19:8-17).

Michal the daughter of Saul whom God used to save David afterwards despised David in heart and became the first and only woman in the Bible who died as a barren woman.

> *"Then David returned to bless his household.*
> *And Michal the daughter of Saul came out to*
> *meet David, and said, how glorious was the king*

*of Israel to day, who uncovered himself to day in
the eyes of the handmaids of his servants, as one
of the vain fellows shamelessly uncovereth
himself! And David said unto Michal, It was
before the LORD, which chose me before thy
father, and before all his house, to appoint me
ruler over the people of the LORD, over Israel:
therefore will I play before the LORD. And I will
yet be more vile than thus, and will be base in
mine own sight: and of the maidservants which
thou hast spoken of, of them shall I be had in
honour. Therefore Michal the daughter of Saul
had no child unto the day of her death" (2
Samuel 6:20-23).*

David, who later became the second king of Israel, served
Saul and behaved wisely wherever he went. Even as a
shepherd boy, he was the one who fought and killed
Goliath. He spared Saul's life, prayed always to know
God's will, but afterwards, committed adultery, hid it,
committed murder, and also numbered Israel in pride.

You have to be warned, as this can happen to anybody any
time. Solomon, the wisest man of his generation who

pleased God so much that God appeared to him many times and granted his (Solomon's) request, afterwards, began to disobey God; married seven hundred wives and had three hundred concubines. In addition, in his old age, they turned his heart away to other gods. So, his heart, which was once perfect with his God, became sinful:

"He did evil also in the sight of the Lord, and went not fully after the Lord. He built a high place Chemosh" (1 Kings 11:7).

Jeroboam was approved by God to rule the northern kingdom of Israel. The king the Lord defended: When King Rehoboam, the son of Solomon, wanted to wage war against him. This same man, King Jeroboam, afterwards, made two calves of gold, one at Bethel and the other he put in Dan, and it became a sin to him. He is today remembered as Jeroboam, the son of Nebat, who made Israel sin against God.

Jehoshaphat was a known king in Israel who walked in the ways of David, his father. He sought the true prophet of God, and did many mighty things for the Lord but later compromised with Ahab and entered into a combined business with a sinner.

*"And after this did Jehoshaphat king of Judah join himself with Ahaziah king of Israel, who did very wickedly: And he joined himself with him to make ships to go to Tarshish: and they made the ships in Ezion–geber. Then Eliezer the son of Dodavah of Mareshah prophesied against Jehoshaphat, saying, Because thou hast joined thyself with Ahaziah, the LORD hath broken thy works. And the ships were broken, that they were not able to go to Tarshish"* (2 Chronicles 20:35-37).

The daughters of Judah, the Zionist daughters, who were once known and recognized in every nation as righteous and holy people, afterwards "began to sew pillows to armholes and make kerchiefs upon the head of every stature to hunt souls (Ezekiel 13:17-19, 22; Hosea 2:13).

Peter the apostle, a man chosen by God, who also received the power to cast out demons, took Jesus to his mother inlaw for healing from fever; who woke Jesus up in their dangerous period to rebuke the storm, a man who vowed never to deny Jesus.

*"But Peter said unto him, although all shall be offended, yet will not I...But he spake the more vehemently, If I should die with thee, I will not deny thee in any wise. Likewise also said they all" (Mark 14:29, 31).*

Peter, who was an eyewitness when Jesus turned water into wine at Cana; a man who saw one of the greatest teachers of the Jews confess to Jesus when he visited Him at night; a man that saw blind Bartimaeus receive his sight during the ministration of Jesus; later began to rebuke Jesus by saying, "Be it far from thee; Lord, this shall not be" (Matt.16:22).

Peter was actually trying to prevent Him (Christ) from going to the cross, which was the purpose for which He came to this world. The same Peter later denied Jesus publicly, saying: "I know not what thou sayest" (Matt. 26:70).

The second time he denied Jesus, saying: "I do not know the man" (Matthew. 26:72).

Finally, the same Peter who walked on the sea and saw all the various miracles performed by Jesus, began to curse and to swear: "I know not the man" (Matthew. 26:74).

How about Judas Iscariot, who is now in hell fire after serving Jesus for three and half-years? He was once a miracle worker among the seventy (Matthew 10:1-4). He preached salvation but never experienced it. He preached forgiveness and confession of sins but when it came to his turn to repent and confess his sins, the enemy stole all he knew about salvation. He forgot that God had never taken and will never take anybody to hell because such a person has sinned.

Judas forgot all the teachings of Jesus to the effect that the only thing that can take a person to hell is one's unwillingness to confess one's sins and forsake them. When he saw that Jesus was condemned, he repented and said to the chief priest and elders: "I have sinned in that I have betrayed the innocent blood" (Matt. 27:4). Instead of repenting, confessing to Jesus and forsaking his sins, he only cast down the pieces of silver in the temple, and went and hanged himself - a terrible mistake! He almost made it but he killed himself; he took away his life and so missed heaven.

How I wished that Judas behaved like the thief on the right hand-side of Jesus when He (Jesus) was on the cross. A man who spent all his time and life serving Satan but in the last hours of his life on earth turned and spoke to his

Creator, who is the greatest man that has ever lived on this earth and said:

> *"...Lord, remember me when thou comest into*
> *thy kingdom..." (Luke 23:39-43).*

No matter how far you have drifted from God, you can still come back to Him. Enoch served Satan for sixty-five years. He begot Methuselah but he walked with God and lived without sin for three hundred years (with sons and daughters). What matters is your decision. In addition, your decision is very important in this regard. Abraham answered the call of God. He left his country, his kindred and his father's house to an unknown place. Jacob was a sup planter but he had an encounter with God. He left Laban by faith, prayed his aggressive brother Esau to reconciliation; and the greatest enemy in his life kissed him (by force). He gave his household the commandment to put away strange gods that were with them, so as to become clean in order to be able to get to Bethel (Genesis 35:1-7).

There is a type of lifestyle you cannot keep if you sincerely desire to get to your real Bethel. You may be a Christian but have settled outside your Bethel. I must get to my Bethel, in the name of Jesus. The serpent in the garden of my life cannot stop me from going to my Bethel, in the name of Jesus. My Cain cannot stop me from going to my Bethel. Marriage cannot stop me from getting to my Bethel. Pharaoh cannot prevent me from reaching my Bethel. The modern Sodom and Gomorrah in the name of church cannot also prevent me from going to my Bethel. Immorality, lying, the Red Sea, Korah, Dathan and Abiram cannot stop me from going to my Bethel. Cozbi or Jezebel cannot equally prevent me from going to my Bethel. Forty two thousand Ephramites could not get to their Bethel simply because they could not pronounce 'Shibboleth.' (Judges 12:5-6).

What is that idol in your life? Take it away from among you because you are going to our Bethel. No argument - just obey the Spirit of God.

Remember what happened to Lot's wife when she disobeyed a divine instruction. The wife of Phinehas died in pain without nursing the baby she called Ichabod, which means that glory has departed from Israel (1 Samuel 4:19-22). Agag died in terrible pain when he never thought of dying. Samuel said:

*"As thy sword hath made women childless, so shall thy mother be childless among women. And he was hewed into pieces before the Lord in Gilgal" (1 Samuel 15:33).*

He never got to his resting place - Bethel.

Goliath (of Gath) was slain by David, a youth of Israel. He never got to his Bethel (1 Samuel 17:49-54).

The archers hit Saul, and he was wounded of the archers. He never got back to his Bethel because he killed himself (1 Chronicles 10:1-7). The young prophet never got to his Bethel –Judah. Lion met him by the way and killed him; and his carcass was cast in the way, and the ass stood by it. The lion also stood by the carcasse. He died in the wrong Bethel when others are running out of Bethel; he took the wrong way, went to the old backslidden prophet and had a meal in a very poor house after rejecting the King's dish. What shame if after all the suffering here on earth, you still miss heaven. Let us go back to our Bethel.

Zimri burnt himself in the house. He never got to his Bethel too (1 Kings 16:18-20). He died in pain. Forty-two children were among the people who suffered pain and died when they abused the man of God. They never came near their Bethel because they died prematurely as they were killed the same day by bears (2 Kings 2:23-24). There was a child who died prematurely too, having been boiled by his mother, who was a witch.

> *"And as the king of Israel was passing by upon the wall, there cried a woman unto him, saying, Help, my lord, O king. And he said, If the LORD do not help thee, whence shall I help thee? Out of the barnfloor, or out of the winepress? And the king said unto her, what aileth thee? And she answered, this woman said unto me, give thy son that we may eat him to day, and we will eat my son to morrow. So we boiled my son, and did eat him: and I said unto her on the next day, Give thy son, that we may eat him: and she hath hid her son" (2 Kings 6:26-29).*

He died under excruciating pain. That child was a victim of eaters of flesh and drinkers of blood. Your sickness, poverty, failure, etc., may be the reason why some other people are rejoicing. Azariah was a king with good prophets around him. He was a king in the nation where

God was doing signs and wonders but he became a leper and died painfully.

> *"And the LORD smote the king, so that he was a leper unto the day of his death, and dwelt in a several house. And Jotham the king's son was over the house, judging the people of the land. And the rest of the acts of Azariah, and all that he did, are they not written in the book of the chronicles of the kings of Judah? So Azariah slept with his fathers; and they buried him with his fathers in the city of David: and Jotham his son reigned in his stead"* (2 Kings 15:5-7).

All city dwellers died under pain because they allowed Menahem to kill them (2 Kings 15:16). A witch or wizard can swallow the destiny of a whole family if the people concerned are not ready to fight. One person in a family can be rich while others are poor (Acts 8:911). If you do not know how to fight your own battle, you may not get to your Bethel. One's own child may even be the person that will kill the person.

*"So Sennacherib king of Assyria departed, and went and returned, and dwelt at Nineveh. And it came to pass, as he was worshipping in the house of Nisroch his god, that Adrammelech and Sharezer his sons smote him with the sword; and they escaped into the land of Armenia: and Esar–haddon his son reigned in his stead"* (Isaiah 37:37-38).

If you do not know how to fight your own battle, your sons, whom you have suffered to raise, may be killed in your presence, before your eyes will be removed. Remember that a little god in your Christian life may prevent you from getting to your Bethel.

*"So they took the king, and brought up to the king of Babylon to Riblah; and they gave judgement upon him. And they slew the sons of Zedekiah before his eyes, and put out the eyes of Zedekiah, and bound him with fetters of brass, and carried him to Babylon"* (2 Kings 25:6-7).

However, my prayer is that it will not be so with you, in the mighty name of Jesus.

You can be a priest (pastor) but with a "little" sin in your life. Things that do not matter so much may take you into captivity. Your enemy may use it to judge you and condemn you.

> *"And the captain of the guard took Seraiah the chief priest, and Zephahiah the second priest, and the three keepers of the door: And out of the city he took an officer that was set over the men of war, and five men; of them that were in the kings presence, which were found in the city, and the principal scribe of the host, which mustered the people of the land"* (2 Kings 25:18-21).

An evil altar is a place of evil storage, a place where captured human progress is stored. Satan is very wicked and destructive but God is very faithful to those who enter into a covenant with Him. He brought the Israelites out of Egypt. Laden with silver and gold and from among their tribes no one faltered. No matter your problem, if you enter into a covenant with God, He will deliver you from all plagues. Disease and sickness will melt away when you confront them with the everlasting word of God (word of covenant).

Sickness, pestilences, fever, poverty, late marriage, inflammation, cancer, heart failure, blindness, madness, ulcer, boils, itching, swellings as well as many other problems came upon the Israelites, who were God's covenant people each time they disobeyed God and despised His covenant with them. However, God always brought healing and deliverance to them whenever they repented, earnestly prayed, and adequately met the covenant conditions (Psalm 107:17-20).

Mercy is one of His (God's) attributes. He has all the power to deliver everyone from every attack and bondage. It is wonderful to know that nothing is impossible with Him. He is the source and possessor of all power. Dynamic power is the power of authority, right, dominion and attorney. The type Jesus gave to His disciples is called power (*dunamis*) and authority (*exousia*), that is, power over all demons and power to destroy disease (Luke 10:1, 19-27).

God's kindness to man, His goodness, mercy, love, forgiveness, and peace, are scattered everywhere in the Bible for all of us. A thorough research in the Bible will reveal to us the abundant love of God for man (John 3:16).

# PRAYER POINTS

## RELEASING THE PRISONERS AT THE EVIL ALTARS

1. Any evil altar banking my destiny; release it by fire by force, in the name of Jesus.

2. Before my time expires, I jump out from evil altars, in the name of Jesus.

3. I move out of my Sodom before the judgment day, in the name of Jesus.

4. Any sin keeping me inside Sodom and Gomorrah; be uprooted by thunder, in the name of Jesus.

5. Angels of God from heaven; take me out from my Sodom, in the name of Jesus.

6. Any evil chain tying me to Sodom and Gomorrah; break by fire, in the name of Jesus.

7. Spirit of delay, delaying me from going out from Sodom and Gomorrah; release me and die, in the name of Jesus.

8. Jehovah Jireh, move my life forward, in the name of Jesus.

9.  I am tired of Sodom. I jump into the ark of my salvation by fire, in the name of Jesus.

10. Any unfriendly friend keeping me back at Sodom; die, in the name of Jesus.

11. My business shall not stand as my God. Oh Lord, deliver me from evil altars, in the name of Jesus.

12. Every altar of immorality destroying in this city; I am not your candidate, in the name of Jesus.

13. Powers from the evil altar aiming at my virginity; die without mercy, in the name of Jesus.

14. Any man, woman, or power that has vowed to hand my blood to demons on the evil altar; die, in the name of Jesus.

15. Any prayer warrior on the evil altar, praying against me; collapse by fire, in the name of Jesus.

16. Any sin in my life ready to hand me over to Satan; be uprooted by thunder, in the name of Jesus.

17. Any blood crying against me from Egypt; close your mouth by the blood of Jesus, in the name of Jesus.

18. Any support given to my enemy from the evil altar; be terminated now, in the name of Jesus.

19. Any man or woman invoking the Egyptian army against my destiny; be frustrated, in the name of Jesus.

20. Oh Lord, trouble my troubles on the evil altars, in the name of Jesus.

21. Oh Lord, remove your help from my enemies, in the name of Jesus.

22. Any power manipulating my life from the evil altars; manipulate your own life, in the name of Jesus.

23. Power of God, pull down any evil altar ministering failure into my life, in the name of Jesus.

24. Any strange fire attacking me from the evil altars; receive the blood of Jesus, in the name of Jesus.

# CHAPTER 8

# GOD'S LOVE AND THE GREAT DECISION

## THE LOVE OF GOD IN EVERY GENERATION

In Genesis 1:26-30, among all the creatures, man is the only one created in the image of God. God further gave man all things, and put him in paradise with all the necessary things. He (God) also visited man often in the Garden of Eden. Man was made to "rule over;" to have absolute authority and control over other creatures. To have authority over our environment and other creatures that are in our planet, we must not bow down for or worship any other creature. Unfortunately, in many African countries and even other parts of the world, many people worship trees, beasts, and birds of the air, water animals and evil spirits.

When his brothers hated Joseph, the Lord loved him and was with him. The Lord was with Joseph everywhere he went so that everywhere he was; he found grace in the sight of the Lord God. He was prospered by God in all he did. The chief butler forgot God remembered Joseph but him; and he was transformed from a prisoner to a prime minister in Egypt. Eventually, his brothers bowed to him (Genesis 43:26).

Joseph's good dreams were all fulfilled and all his eleven brothers bowed to him. Do not give up because all your enemies will eventually bow to you (Genesis 44:14, 16-33). Therefore, Joseph was more highly elevated than his brothers were. He later was reunited with his father's family, and they all settled down to enjoy the best of Egypt. The Lord gave him the heathen for an inheritance. He gave him the treasures of darkness; the riches stored in secret places. He fulfilled his destiny and died at an old age after seeing his children's children.

When would you like to die? At what age would you like to die and how will you go? Will you allow the evil altars in your village to terminate your life? Joseph overcame all the terrible household wickedness against it both at home and abroad, i.e. local and international. At home, Joseph was an over comer; and away from home, he was an over comer. That was because he availed himself of the grace of God to prevail over his life (Titus 2:11-12).

In Exodus, God showed his love greatly to the Israelites, just as he is doing today to all Christians. He multiplied the seed of Israel anywhere the people were found - in Egypt and outside Egypt. He gave their women "easy delivery. He spared Moses' life, which was later used mightily by Him. God also confronted their archenemy, Pharaoh, and killed him and his hosts (Exodus 2:23).

He (God) also destroyed all those who were after the life of Moses (Exodus 4:19). God had to kill all the firstborn of Egypt just to save His own people (Exodus 11:29, 30). He (God) overthrew the Egyptian army in the midst of the sea just to demonstrate the love he had for his own people. What you just need is to be God's own person and He will always fight for you. He gave the Israelites favour in the sight of the Egyptians. How marvellous will it be when all your enemies open their eyes wide and see God's goodness all over you? Do not die because the impossibility in your life will soon become possible.

When the water of the people of Israel became bitter for three days, the Lord dropped invisible "sugar" into the water and "healed" the water. God "treated" the water. Do not give up because your own package of blessing is on the way. Your life will experience sweetness again (Exodus 22:23, 25-26). That "sugar" is Jesus. When the Israelites needed food, God rained manna from the heavenly kitchen, and for forty years, they were eating like kings, queens, princes and princesses in the wilderness. He also gave them water where there was no water.

Joshua was used to lead them in their first battle and they defeated the people of Amalek (Exodus 17:1-16). In Leviticus, the Lord spoke to defend the poor hired servants (Leviticus 19:13). A poor but wise person can become rich with his wages.

In the Book of Numbers, He remembered and showed His love to the daughters of Zelophehad (Numbers 27:1-11). In Deuteronomy God remembered the fatherless in love and gave commandments in their favour (Deuteronomy 24:16, 17-22). He also included the widows and strangers in his love and care for humankind.

In the Book of Joshua, He delivered a prostitute, Rehab (Joshua 6:22-23, 25). Wherever you are on any evil altar, the Lord can still visit you. No matter how sinful, sick or troubled you are, He can still reach you.

In the Book of Judges, the children of Israel were delivered when they cried unto God. You can also be delivered if only you will sincerely cry to God (Judges 3:5-9).

In the Book of Ruth, God visited Bethlehem within the tribe of Judah and gave them bread (Ruth 1:6-7). God will surely visit you (This is a prophecy); and when He visits you, demand more than bread. You can ask for anything you want and it shall be given to you. In the Book of 1 Samuel, Eleazer was sanctified and set aside to keep the ark of God. That was God's mercy. Is there anything you are keeping for God? What do you want, and what is your ambition in this life? (1 Samuel 7:1-2). It was the mercy of God what made Abiathar escape death. You can also escape your problem. The end has not come; you can still make it in this life despite all odds (1 Samuel 22:20-23).

Out of God's grace, an Egyptian received God's mercy. His problems were solved and sickness was removed. David fed him and he possibly became an Israelite. You can become anything you want to be provided you are ready to fight all evil altars (1 Samuel 30:11-16).

In the Book of 2 Samuel, Saul's men "waxed weaker while David's men became stronger. If you are where you are not supposed to be, you will soon lose every battle even if you are winning now. So join the righteous camp and you will become a strong soldier of God (2 Samuel 3:1-21).

In the Book of 1 Kings, Elijah, the prophet of God, who confronted the false prophets of Baal at Mount Carmel, was saved from a witch; the greatest harlot of her generation who was called Jezebel; a woman that called herself a prophetess. This woman's spirit has destroyed many ministers and is still destroying many people today. The spirit of Jezebel is still doing the same work today (1 Kings 19:1-5).

By the mercy of God, Elisha received a double portion of Elijah's power (2 Kings 2:1-25). Whatever you need today, the Lord can double it for you. With the double portion of his master's power, Elisha performed many miracles - multiplied oil for a woman of faith and that woman became the first woman to own an oil company in her generation. With the same double portion of anointing, Elisha was able to feed the sons of the prophets (2 Kings 4:34-44). He later became an instrument in the hands of God that healed Naaman of his leprosy, defeated the whole Assyrian army without even a gun, causing all their great soldiers to become blind in a moment (2 Kings 6:1-23).

Elisha was one of the greatest prophets. He prophesied from his sickbed; and even many years after his death and burial, his bones raised the dead (2 Kings 13:14-21). With "a double portion" anointing, much more can take place. What more are you waiting for? Why don't you ask for double portion anointing?

In 1 Chronicles, the sons of Asaph were separated for music. What are you separated for? (1 Chronicles 25:1-2). Shielomith and his brothers were in charge of the dedicated things. What are the things you are in charge of? (1 Chronicles 26:20-28). The Izharites were in charge of outward business over Israel, for officers and judges (1 Chronicles 26:29). The Hebronites were in charge of the business of the western part of Israel; they were mighty men (1 Chronicles 26:30-37). Why are you in the body of Christ? Which part are you occupying in Him? Are you a pillar or a caterpillar in the church of Christ? Remember that the wages of sin is death and that the soul that sins shall die, as clearly indicated in Bible.

In the Book of 2 Chronicles, the Lord appeared to Solomon and gave him wisdom, understanding and knowledge (2 Chronicles 1:7-17). You say that you are born again, but when God appeared to you, what did He give you? If truly you have had an encounter with Christ, He must have given you something (Ephesians 4:11-12).

In the Book of Ezra, God restored the children of Israel to their land of promise after seventy years and the Lord's temple was built again. You are the temple of God and once you repent, He is ready to drive the enemies out of your life, heal you, deliver you, and make you whole. No matter how long the enemy has occupied the womb, brain, blood and other organs of your body, the Lord can still drive them out of your life (Ezra 1:1-11, 3:8-13).

Nehemiah, by the mercy of God, received favour from the king, who gave a letter of authority to build and repair the gate of Jerusalem (Nehemiah 2:1-20; 5:14-19). The demons in the gate of your life, family, business, profession, etc., can be driven away as soon as you begin to pray in righteousness. Just destroy the evil gate built by your ancestors and erect a good one. When one decides for Christ, begins to live a holy life and prays in faith, he is building a new gate.

Is there any sin that is still reigning in your life? That is an evil gate. Have you been raped? That is an evil gate. Are you vile? That is an evil gate. Are you a murderer? That is an evil gate. Do you practice magical arts? That is also an evil gate. Are you an idol worshipper? That is an evil gate. Do you belong to any secret cult? That also is an evil gate. Are you a liar? That is also an evil gate as well.

Are you greedy and depraved? That is an evil gate. Are you envious of other people's progress? That is also an evil gate. Are you a deceiver? That is also an evil gate. Do you steal? That is an evil gate.

Do you know that deceit, malice, gossip, slander, hatred, bad language, arrogance, pride, etc., have taken many to hell? If you become proud, faithless, ruthless, heartless, etc., you open an evil gate for demons to come in and attack you. The scripture does not keep us in ignorance of the devil (Galatians 5:19-21).

God has given everybody who is born again a letter of authority, which is better than the one given to Nehemiah to build a better gate (John 1:12).

In the Book of Esther, God delivered the Jews from an evil decree. When you are delivered from evil decree, promotion must become your portion. Your Haman must die in your place. The curses placed on you must be reversed. To get the blessing of Esther, begin to reveal the plot of the devil against God, the church, and believers. Take a firm decision not to bow to Haman, rather mourn, pray, and fast as never before. Involve all the Esther's around you to take a radical decision to approach the King of kings.

Once you start praying, make sure you lift holy hands and not dirty ones; not hands that have shed blood, or touched unholy things. Lift holy hands and the King of kings, who neither slumbers nor sleeps will remember you. Your file appears for promotion above your Haman, who will definitely be swallowed by his evil plots against you. In the Book of Job, we saw a wonderful picture of deliverance from the spirit of impossibility.

An unforgiving spirit has robbed many people of their great blessings. God refused to restore fully the blessings of Job until he prayed for some people. There are people you must pray for before you can fully be delivered. The concerned person may be somebody you have vowed never to forgive. There are people who are praying and fasting, doing all manner of Christian service; but as long as they still hate somebody, they may never get their requests granted (Job 42:10-12).

It seems that many are not interested in the love of God for this generation. The people of Sodom and Gomorrah despised God's mercy and love and God destroyed them. The generation of Noah also despised the mercy of God, and as a result, God wiped it out with a flood. Again, God destroyed every living substance on the surface of the earth.

The host of the army of Egypt was destroyed because nobody was out to stand for them. In the prophetic dispensation, God in the Book of Isaiah advised the righteous to fully separate themselves from sinners and stay with God (Isaiah 8:11-22; 9:1-7; 10:20-24; 29:18-24).

In the Book of Jeremiah, God in His mercy, visited the house of the Rechabites with a promise that they would not want a man to stand before God forever (Jeremiah 35:1-19). In addition, in the Book of Ezekiel, God in His love warned the false builders to stop their evil building (Ezekiel 13:13-16). In the book of Daniel, God brought salvation, deliverance and true worship in Babylon through three young men from Hebrew land, and

191 • Prayer M. Madueke

promoted them. These three young men were, Shedrack, Meshack and Abednego (Daniel 3:1-30).

In the Book of Matthew, i.e. in the New Testament dispensation, God demonstrated His love through His only begotten Son by the power of the Holy Ghost and helped all that believed. He healed all manner of sicknesses and diseases; including demonic cases (Matthew 4:23-25).

In the Book of Mark, the mercy of God was made visible when a man with an unclean spirit was delivered, as Jesus said to the demons, "Hold thy peace and come out of him" (Mark 1:23-29).

Again, in the gospel according to Saint Luke, a dead man carried out of the city for burial; the only son of his mother, who was also a widow, was resurrected by Jesus, when He confronted the woman and turned to the dead body and said: "Young man, I say unto thee, arise (Luke 7:11-17).

When Jesus met the poor who were very hungry, having followed Him for a long time without food, He fed five thousand men (besides women and children) with only five loaves and two fishes. Afterwards, twelve baskets were gathered as leftover (John 6:514).

In the Acts of the Apostles, Aeneas, sick of palsy, was saved and healed, and his palsy disappeared by fire (Acts 9:32-35).

The mercy of God can be seen in all generations. That is the reason He is called Jehovah Shammah, the Lord who is present to help us (Ezekiel 48:35). God is also called Jehovah-Jireh; which means, the Lord will provide (Genesis 22:13-14).

Our God is able to provide anything we need. At His command, the fish, which swallowed Jonah, vomited him from the chambers of the queen of the coast. No evil altar can be so stubborn as to hold you when you confront it with the blood of Jesus. You can be delivered, no matter your condition. What you need now is God.

When man was created in the image of God, he initially walked in innocence, holiness and righteousness, but he later voluntarily drifted from God. That is the reason why every man is totally inclined to evil. However, God does not want us to remain in that state, so He planned for our redemption. He sent the only One, who was capable of redeeming us. Therefore, Jesus came and died in our place.

What we now need is to repent of all sins. That is, to turn from all sins and have a change of heart and attitude. Once you repent and do all your restitutions, you are then ready for battle. The Lord has been waiting for you all these years. Your life cannot continue like that. There must be a change for the better. All evil altars operating against you must be destroyed. With God all things are possible (Mark 9:23).

If you are a sinner, you are not the worst sinner. If you have problems, yours are not the worst either. Even if your sins and problems are the worst, God, who can turn the worst to the best, is ever ready to deliver you.

**Manasseh** (2 Chronicles 33:1-6, 7, 11-13, 15-16)

Manasseh who was the wicked king in Judah reigned for fifty-five years. He did evil before God. His sins and abominations were like that of the land of Canaan:

1.  He built again the high places which Hezekiah his father had broken.

2.  He made altars for Baalim.

3.  He made groves.

4.    He worshipped and served all the hosts of heaven right in the two courts of the house of the Lord.

5.    In addition, he built altars for all the hosts of the heaven right in the two courts of the house of the Lord.

6.    He caused his children to pass through fire in the valley of the son of Hinnom.

7.    He observed times.

8.    He made enchantments.

9.    He used witchcraft.

10.   He associated with familiar spirits and wizards.

11.   He wrought much evil in the sight of the Lord to provoke Him to anger.

12.   He set a carved image, i.e. the idol, which he made in the house of God.

13.   He made Judah, the inhabitants of Jerusalem err, and do worse things than the heathen whom the Lord had destroyed before the children of Israel (were given the land).

14.   The Lord spoke to him and his people but they would not listen.

15. He made altars for Baal and made a grove, as did Ahab King of Israel.

16. He shed innocent blood so much that he filled Jerusalem from one end to another (2 Kings 21:16).

Titus Flavius Josephus, first-century Romano Jewish scholar, historian and hagiographer, said that he did not even spare the prophets. It is a view held by many that he (Manasseh) even killed Isaiah, the prophet. What an abomination! He offered his children to Molech in the valley of the son of Hinnom. That is what the scripture means when it says that Manasseh caused his children to pass through fire. What he did was never before done in Judah.

Manasseh was to say the least, characteristized by high-class acts of wickedness. He was very brutal and thirsty for blood. Therefore, he attached no value to human life. In addition, because of these sins, Manasseh entered into great trouble. He was allowed by God to be arrested by the captains of the hosts of Assyria. They took him among the thorns, bound him with fetters, and carried him to Babylon. He must have spent time (while in his affliction) making incantations and invoking his gods (Kings 18:26-29).

Manasseh served Satan very deeply and at the time he needed Satan most, Satan disappointed him. If Satan disappointed the people that served him most who else will he not disappoint? It was at this point that Manasseh was convinced that Satan was not and will never be a friend to anyone. Nobody can bring out friendship from where God Himself has put enmity (Genesis 3:15).

If you are occultist, Manasseh, I suppose, was more cultic. If you are abominable, I think Manasseh was more abominable. If you are wicked, Manasseh, I suppose, was wicked. Nobody (from Genesis to Revelation and from generation to generation) has ever prospered to the end in serving Satan.

The people of Sodom and Gomorrah tried and failed and you will therefore not succeed. (Genesis 18:16, 20; 19:5-9). Pharaoh, himself tried and failed. In fact nobody will succeed (Exodus 1:10-16). The man of mixed blood (Egypt and Israel) failed. So how do you think you will succeed (Leviticus 24:10-16, 23)? The congregation of Israel failed. Do not think you will ever succeed in serving the devil (Numbers 16:41-50).

The five kings on the coasts of Jordan tried to oppose God but they all failed. So why are you trying to do what five great kings could not do (Joshua 9:1-2)? Even Samson tried it and lost his two eyes. He was imprisoned by common people, and later died with his enemies in a strange land (Judges 16:1, 4-7).

Ahitophel and Absalom also failed, so you will not just succeed. Even Satan himself opposed God and failed. So why do you think you will succeed? Who are you to succeed without God (Revelation 20:7, 43)? Manasseh fought God and His people with all his strength, but when he could no more go ahead, he surrendered to God with all his heart. To fight God unto death is the greatest mistake any man or woman can make (2 Chronicles 33:11-13).

Only the mercy of God can work on a man like Manasseh. He did repent and served God faithfully with all his heart. King Saul, Solomon, Uzziah and many other kings started their reign in a good way but ended very badly. However, Manasseh started very badly and ended very well. You may be a very wicked person but you can change. If God accepted Manasseh when he humbled himself greatly and prayed unto Him, He (God) will also accept you if you do the same thing. Who can battle with the Lord? Nobody!

Not even Satan can do so. Manasseh was one among many who fought a good battle. To fight a good battle, you must humble yourself before God, accept, and pray to the only true God.

In the Book of Samuel 15, Saul disobeyed God's commandment. That day Samuel, the prophet of God, said to him: "I will not return with thee for thou hast rejected the word of the Lord, and God hath rejected thee from being king over Israel"(1 Samuel 15:26).

If God has rejected somebody, do not accept that person. In the family of Saul and Israel as a whole, only Jonathan, Saul's first son, was able to openly confront Saul. From the day Jonathan saw the spirit of God in David, he loved David.

Though his father and all the members of his household hated David, Jonathan loved him (Samuel 18:1-4). When Jonathan discovered that his father was determined to kill David he revealed it to David and thus spared his life (Samuel 19:4-5). Jonathan disagreed with his father but he did that respectfully. Jonathan entered into a covenant with the house of David forever (1 Samuel 20:14-17, 29-34, 42).

There was no manner of curse that Saul did not pronounce upon his first son, Jonathan, because he stood with God. Probably, all the younger brothers and sisters of Jonathan joined their father in cursing Jonathan. I do not know why Jonathan died prematurely but I do know that parental curse could be disastrous if not fought against.

However, God stood behind Jonathan in life and in death. Jonathan disagreed with his father but he always did that very respectfully. Jonathan's pleaded for David. Jonathan spoke well of David unto Saul, his father, and said:

> *"Let not the king sin against his servant David because David has not sinned against you. His works have always been very good. He risked his life and slew Goliath the giant. The Lord brought great victory and salvation to Israel through him and you saw it and rejoiced. Wherefore then will thou sin against innocent blood to slay David without a reason? Why should David be killed? What has he done?" (1 Samuel 20:32)*

In addition, in verse 34, Jonathan was openly angry because of his father's sins. He fasted for his father's sins and for the security of David's life. In addition, while

Jonathan was going through abuses and persecutions for standing for righteousness, all his brothers, sisters, and all the members of Saul's family were enjoying evil. They knew that Saul was doing evil but they failed to confront him.

Jonathan, on his own part, used every available means to appeal to his father to follow the path of righteousness, an appeal from son to father in the most respectful manner. Nevertheless, Saul would not heed his appeal. Jonathan justified and cleared David of any wrongdoing, and indicted his father, Saul, of extreme selfishness, jealousy, treachery etc. Jonathan told his father that David was a good example to follow. His defense for David was most touching. He presented David as a man of God; a true patriot who had risked his life for the good of his people, and saved them in a desperate crisis.

Jonathan sought the truth of the matter between his father and David and defended the truth. When Jonathan saw his father's evil intentions against David, he became ashamed of his father. He realized that his father was once a godly man, who confessed his sins and had a changed heart. Once he was filled with the Holy Spirit; a godly and dedicated man that humbled himself before God. He was always used by God to do many mighty things. He prophesied and brought victories to the whole nation. Nevertheless, he later became depraved, backslidden and ungodly; and took sides with Satan and the defeated. When Jonathan examined and proved his father backslidden, though still a king in control of the whole nation (Israel), he could neither eat nor drink, even during festive days. He prayed and mourned for his father, Saul.

When your father, mother, friend, manager, child, husband, wife, head of department etc., begins to drift from the truth, how do you handle the situation? Adam did not resist Eve when she gave him the forbidden fruit. He ate the fruit and that is the reason the whole world is under a curse today.

When the men of Sodom and Gomorrah began to practice wickedness. Lot singled himself out. When your parents become Miriam and Aaron, and begin to speak against their pastor, church leaders, or anybody else, do you join them? You should not, because that will amount to sin. The congregation of Israel wept, murmured, blamed Moses and God, and even planned to go back to Egypt, i.e. old (sinful) fellowship. Remember that God prevented all of them from seeing the Promised Land, let alone entering it. They all died in the wilderness and their children wandered in the wilderness of life for a total of forty years instead of forty days.

Do not join your parents to worship idols. Remember also Koran, Dathan and Abiram and all the renowned men of Israel. The earth opened and swallowed them alive, with their property and members of their families, who refused to talk to their parents (or husbands) when they were opposing Moses and Aaron. There are many idol worshippers today in the church. When you cannot confront your parents, who are opposed to divinely constituted authority in the church, you make them idols.

If as a pastor or leader you cannot allow your members to talk to you, discipline, or rebuke you with the Bible, you are a human altar, who will soon die with your church members and family, as in the case of Achan or Jezebel.

Thanks be to God for a man like Jonathan who is a very good example in this regard. A man that could say: "Daddy, you are wrong in this matter," but with respect. He was a man that could live in the house of a king but will refuse to eat the King's food, a man who could go into fasting while there was a lot of good food. God is looking for those who can stand before the mighty altar of Nebuchadnezzar and declare before the king and in the presence of all the princes, governors, captains, judges, treasurers, councilors, chiefs and all the rulers of provinces that they will not serve other gods except the only true God. God is looking for such people in every family, school, office, market and in every generation.

Jonathan died and David wept for him and commanded Israel to mourn his death (2 Samuel 1:13-27). Although Jonathan died, David showed kindness to all those who were left in his house for his sake (2 Samuel 9:3-13). He restored all that had been lost in the house of Saul to Mephibosheth, the son of Jonathan, the son of Saul.

Curses that were rained upon Jonathan by his father, Saul, almost wiped all the children of Jonathan away except a lame man. Righteousness alone may not exterminate a curse. We need righteousness, the right prayer points, and continued faith in Christ to fight to the end, both parental and all other curses (2 Samuel 19:24-30).

Even if you are lame, you can still make it, if only you will begin to lay a good foundation like Jonathan. When there was a judgement that seven men must die in the house of Saul after three years of devastating famine in the land, the righteous foundation laid by Jonathan spared his son, Mephibosheth. Not all his other family members who survived the famine and other problems in Israel were spared. Those who did not die lost their children on the day of the harvest. It is a disappointment to die on the day of the harvest. They were handed over to their archenemy and were later hanged on the hill (2 Samuel 21:6-9).

Mephibosheth, the son of Jonathan, might be lame, illiterate, sickly, poor, etc., but death, or eaters of flesh and drinkers of blood would not touch him because of his father's good foundation. King Saul had a bad foundation. However, Jonathan laid a good foundation for himself and for his lineage. Covenants made on evil altars are for the children already born and those yet unborn - for all generations.

Our ancestors, standing on their evil altars many years ago, entered into covenants with unseen evil spirits and these covenants are affecting many of us today. Moreover, they will continue to affect many people unless something is done to separate us from them, i.e. those evil covenants. Therefore, unless you stand out like Jonathan and Abraham, you must face evil and stubborn pursuers from evil altars. Their commitments to evil spirits on evil altars are irrevocable unless Christ is involved. Thanks be to God also that there are women on the list, like the woman of Shunem.

# THE SHUNAMMITE WOMAN

*"And it fell on a day, that Elisha passed to Shunem, where was a great woman; and she constrained him to eat bread. And so it was, that as oft as he passed by, he turned in thither to eat bread. And she said unto her husband, Behold now, I perceive that this is an holy man of God, which passeth by us continually. Let us make a little chamber, I pray thee, on the wall; and let us set for him there a bed, and a table, and a stool, and a candlestick: and it shall be, when he cometh to us that he shall turn in thither. And it fell on a day, that he came thither, and he turned into the chamber, and lay there. And he said to Gehazi his servant, Call this Shunammite. And when he had called her, she stood before him"* (2 Kings 4:8-12).

The Shunammite woman was great in every sense; highly placed, rich, noble etc. She invited the prophet into her house. Have you given Jesus an invitation to sup with you? Your body is the temple of the Holy Spirit. This woman had no child but when she met the greatest prophet of her time, she conceived and bore a son according to the prophetic utterance of Elisha. Jesus Christ is the Creator of Elisha, a greater and better prophet than all the prophets in the whole Bible. This woman manifested "Faith in action" when she confronted death, which had snatched her only son

Among these women of God also was the wife of the sons of the prophets. She knew her rights when she excused herself from her husband's creditors, who came to take her two sons as bondservants or slaves. Moreover, after her discussion with the prophet, she came back and paid all her husband's debts, and by faith became the first woman in the Bible who had oil Company. Her children also lived and enjoyed life in abundance (2 Kings 4:1-7).

Do not allow your child to die. Go out in faith and meet the greatest prophet of all ages, the Lord Jesus Christ. What more can I say? For time will fail me to talk about Mary and Martha who lost their only brother, but because they invited Christ, a miracle still took place in the grave. They, having invited the "resurrection and life," Lazarus jumped out of the grave.

How about Jabez? The scripture has the answer in 1 Chronicles 4:9-10. God will grant you your request only if you are ready to repent and forsake your sins and your fathers' evil altars.

Job started resisting the devil very late. He was initially deceived by thinking that only righteousness without the right knowledge could set him free (James 4:7). He spent much time talking to the day he was born, and the night he was conceived. Job did not know that he might have been conceived in broad daylight while he was busy addressing the night of his own imagination. Job with all his righteousness went on to talk to things he ought not to talk to, thereby leaving his enemy at work upon his flesh (Job 3:11-12).

The enemy may allow you to go to the wrong place, pray the wrong prayers, and do other wrong things, even with your righteousness. He actually likes it that way. Thanks be to God because Job later acknowledged God, got healed and was delivered. Nevertheless, he really suffered. I want deliverance but not like Job; I want it now.

Even if you are a witch or wizard, is your own witchcraft greater than that of Simon the sorcerer, who bewitched a whole nation but was delivered when he turned to the

Lord? (Acts 8:9-24). A man called Bar-Jesus was also delivered because he took the right step (Acts 13:6-12).

If you are stubborn, you may not be more stubborn than Jonah, who heard the voice of God very clearly and still rejected God's instructions. Jonah thought he could run away from God but everywhere he ran to, God was already there waiting for him; to welcome him with love.

Where are you now? Are you in the church, grave, inside a tree etc? Where are you? Are you in the house of a native doctor (or herbalist)? Are you presently in the worst condition? Take the right step and secure your freedom and deliverance.

Jesus met a young man, the only son of his widowed mother, dead, outside the city gate. Jesus Himself with His disciples confronted death with life and it became a matter of life versus death. When the two powers clashed, the lesser power bowed to the higher one! Jesus, the Prince of life, just said: "Woman, weep not. Young men, I say to thee, arise" And the miracle took place. Are you a widow? Just surrender to Jesus.

When Jonah refused deliverance and chose to be stubborn, God prepared a fish for him. The fish then swallowed him. Nevertheless, Jonah in his stubbornness resisted until the third day before he repented. The miracle took place immediately. You cannot be more stubborn than Jonah can.

Finally, let us examine our father of faith - Abraham. He left his father's foundation and built a new one. He believed in God. You can also believe in God today (Isaiah 51:1- 2). He started life in uncertainty; but because God was involved, he succeeded and today, he is "the father of faith. There were people who fought their battles in the Bible. Many are fighting theirs now. You can start your own battle today (1 Timothy 6:12; 2 Timothy 4:6-8; Mark 9:23).

Evil altars can be destroyed, physically or spiritually. You may not have the opportunity to destroy your father's evil altars physically but wherever you are now, you can (also point your finger to the direction of your place of birth or the location of the evil altars) speak to the evil altars by faith with a view to destroying them. Plead the blood of Jesus Christ seven times with a loud voice to raise a good altar against the evil altars you have destroyed by faith (Judges 6:25-26).

Building upon the Rock means doing everything from today according to the word of God. Do everything from today in an ordered way. Do not misplace your priorities, and do not compromise with sin. Do everything according to God's will. Do not ever be in haste again. We must succeed by the grace of God and according to the will of God. Do anything worth doing in the right way and in the ordered way, place and time. In addition, once you lose that time, you may need an extra battle to recover it fully. There is also a time to die - a time that every problem in your life ought to die. Once you discover that fire, do not use it for any other thing.

Spend all your energy and time to kill things that need to be killed in your life; time to kill every evil altar's deposit in your life, namely, barrenness, poverty, premature death, cancer, ulcer, late or no marriage, spiritual evil marks, and any other problems from the evil altar. If you allow that time to pass, your destiny may not be fulfilled.

Once you read the word of God, or you receive the vision of God's will for your life, you have to fight with every available weapon. Do not spare the problems; do not use the time to kill to save. If it is a time to plant, do not waste time; do not allow manipulation. Building in the ordered place means understanding the seasons and times set aside by God for every purpose under heaven. It means knowing the time to be born. Do not allow the enemy to prolong your labour; do not give birth before or after the time.

Do not under-stay or overstay in any programme. Discover the time to plant, and plant exactly at that time. Know the time to harvest, and use it for that purpose. If you have to kill, kill. There is a time to kill and a time to heal. There is also a time to break down and a time to build up. There is also a time to weep, and a time to laugh. Do not laugh when you are supposed to weep and, vice versa. Discover the time for everything and make use of each season properly (Ecclesiastes 3:1-8).

There was a man whose conception, birth and ministry were announced by an angel but he did not use his divine timetable and programme sheet very well. He allowed a small marine spirited girl to amputate his destiny He died in regret asking Jesus: "Are you the person who was to come or do we look for another." What an insult! This was the same man who testified before many when he said: "Behold the lamb of God, which taketh away the sins of the world. I knew him not: but he that sent me" (John 1:29, 33-37, 45).

This same John the Baptist suffered in prison. If some believers were meant to be locked up in the prison, it should not be John the Baptist. If you are complaining that you are imprisoned because of your faith in Christ, bear in mind that you are not supposed to die there. If you are not happy to suffer and die for Christ anywhere you are, you are not supposed to be there. It is good to die for Christ's sake but if you are dying, complaining, and almost finding fault with Christ for not saving you, it is either you have backslidden, not born again at all, or you allowed a lesser power to handle your case.

If we must suffer for Christ, it must be with joy. If you have lost your relationship with Christ because of a particular problem in your life, that problem is not meant to overcome you. Any problem that Christ Himself allows in your life must not take you to hell. What I mean is that the problem will be used to accomplish God's purpose in your life. I do not mean sickness or demons, but problems that God may allow in your life to accomplish your ministry and give glory to Him.

Therefore, if God takes you to prison like John the Baptist, it is to help you fulfil your ministry. If John the Baptist was not discouraged, perhaps an angel of the Lord God Almighty would have come down to help him, even inside the prison. Alternatively, he would have just disappeared and Herod would be confused; and the fear of God would have come upon the whole city. Nevertheless, we lost our John to a small marine-spirited girl and her mother, an adulterous. Our beloved John died; a man whose conception and birth an angel announced; a man that God said should bring joy and gladness in Israel.

Nevertheless, those who rejoiced at his birth were still alive to weep when he died and the head of a great prophet was displayed by a small girl who was an agent of Satan (Luke 1:14). John the Baptist, a great man of God, a man filled with the Holy Ghost from his mother's womb, died; and many that would have turned to the Lord were discouraged when they saw how he died. They expected him not to die that way but he did not use the power made available to him (Luke 1:17). What a great ministry he bad, but he died prerpaturely in the hands of an agent of Satan, a home breaker, and an adulterous (Matthew 11:2, 6).

Herod locked up the "spirit and power of Elijah." And this was what Ahab and his wife Jezebel failed to do; what four hundred and fifty prophets of Baal could not do throughout their lives; what famine could not do for years, and what death has failed to do up until now. Is your life locked up on any evil altar? Is your marriage locked up in the prison of evil altars? Is your destiny locked up on any evil altar prison?

An evil altar is a satanic prison-yard but you can break out now! Are you ready? If your answer is yes, then get ready to come out now. We are not going to fight with the spirit of Elijah but with the Spirit of Jesus Christ, our deliverer. This was the Spirit that healed all manner of sickness and disease in the lives of people while teaching and preaching the gospel of the kingdom (Matthew 4:23-25). This was the Spirit that said, "I will, be thou clean," and leprosy vanished just in a moment of time (Matthew. 8:3).

The same Spirit said to a centurion:

"Go thy way, and as thou has believed, so be it done unto thee" (Matthew. 8:13).

This Spirit commanded the evil spirit in a man and said, "Hold thy peace and come out of him..." (Luke 4:35)

He also said to a man sick of the palsy, "Son, thy sin be forgiven thee. Arise; take up thy bed and go" (Mark 2:3-12).

In addition, this Spirit calmed the great storm in the lives of the apostles by just saying: "Peace, be still" (Mark 4:39).

He is the same Spirit that every believer has received from the Lord Jesus at repentance. The same Spirit encountered a woman who had an issue of blood for twelve years and said: "Daughter, thy faith hath made thee whole of thy plague. Go in peace and be whole" (Mark 5:34).

Are you sick? Allow the Spirit of Christ to initiate and perfect your healing. This was also the spirit that encountered a virgin and she conceived the greatest man of all generations - past, present and future. This Spirit removed the barrenness of Elizabeth.

When this Spirit met men who were fed up with life - defeated individuals who had toiled all night yet without success - he told them: "Fear not, for from henceforth, thou shall catch more than fish."

The same Spirit told a woman who had just lost her only son: "Weep not." He cast out seven spirits from Mary Magdalene and she became whole. He fed five thousand hungry men with only five small loaves of bread and two small fishes. He healed an impotent man who had the spirit of infirmity for thirty-eight years with only a statement: "Rise, take up thy bed and walk" (John 5:8).

Today, you can walk out of every evil situation and no evil altar can hold you again. You have a better opportunity than John the Baptist does.

> *"Verily I say unto you, among them that are born of women there hath not risen a greater than John the Baptist: notwithstanding he that is least in the kingdom of heaven is greater than he."* (<u>Matthew 11:11</u>)

The problem with John the Baptist was that he did not resist the arrester, who was Herod the Tetrarch. If John had commanded fire from heaven, who was Herod to lay an evil hand on a man with fire? Which kind of prison would have locked John if he had acted as God had expected him to? Jesus will allow you to die in your prison, if the only thing you can do is just to ask unnecessary questions and complain like John the Baptist.

Imagine Herod binding John the Baptist. The thing that is now binding your marriage, destiny, etc., may be weaker than what Herod used to bind John the Baptist with. The altar that a witch or wizard is using against your business, promotion, marriage etc., may be weaker than what Herod used against John the Baptist, who allowed himself to be bound. Who was Herodias, and who was her daughter to have terminated the life of John the Baptist? It is a pity that John the Baptist allowed his life to be sacrificed as a birthday gift to an agent of Satan, the devil.

Do not allow your mother, father, "friend," colleague, enemy, etc., to submit or donate you to their cultic group. Fight it out with such a demonic person through aggressive fire prayers. If you know the Spirit working in you, as a Christian, you will never allow your head to enter into a charger of a demonic girl. Where is your health now? Is it in Herod's daughter's charger? Where is your marriage, destiny, children etc.? Though John the Baptist was buried, it was only his headless body that was recovered and buried by his disciples. It was a very pitiful situation.

If you must die before the rapture, do not allow Herod to kill you. If you should remain unmarried, let it not be because an evil altar is holding your marriage. Solomon allowed women to destroy him. Samson allowed Delilah to destroy him in the land of Philistines. Abel allowed Cain (his brother) to destroy him even when God had said some good things concerning him. Lot allowed drunkenness to overcome him; and his two daughters committed immorality with him. Balaam allowed covetousness to control him, and he lost his ministry as a result.

The other ten men who spied the land with Joshua and Caleb allowed fear to destroy them. If you die in your situation, you will not have anybody to blame. No evil altar can withstand a true and knowledgeable battle-ready child of God. You can jump out of any evil altar that has been holding you captive; and thus, become a free child of God, conscious of your rights in the Lord and Savior Jesus Christ.

I met a man who had lived in Rome for twelve years, where he obtained a master's degree before he became a prosperous international businessperson. His late grandfather was a dangerous occultist and a powerful native doctor, who was feared by all in the town. This man, it was said, was fortified demonically. Those who had seen him make some spectacular demonstration of his powers also knew him. This man, I learnt, sent for all his children and grandchildren before his death. He narrated his encounters with people; his relationships and covenants with evil powers. He reminded them of his fame in occultism.

After that, he took them back of his house, demanded for all his cultic materials, and got all of them burnt. He warned his children and grandchildren never to engage in anything cultic. He enlightened them on the advantages and disadvantages of occultism. After that, he died. Unfortunately, his children and grandchildren never regarded his words but went into the same evil practice. One of this occult man's grandsons, though aware of all these things, went ahead and became more cultic than his grandfather was (Daniel 5:22-27).

He became a very wealthy young man who was travelling from one European country to another. Though he was rich, he had the mark of non-achievement. With all his money, he still failed to achieve any reasonable thing. He got deeply involved in drug trafficking, and made a lot of money through it. After visiting Nigeria at a certain time, when he went back to Italy, his ancestral spirit travelled with him. Right there in one of the streets of Italy, a huge and powerful personality appeared to him and guided him back to his residence there (in Italy), and commanded him to take his portfolio and rush to the airport.

This ancestral spirit in the form of a human being, who was invisible to other people, took him to the airport where he obtained a flight ticket back to Nigeria. When I met him, he had been in Nigeria for ten years, with a good master's degree from one of the best universities in Italy, yet without a job. He had also married and divorced six women, including a senior army officer within the period (ten years) and was living with the seventh wife who had a small boy for him.

He was so confused and dejected that he went from one pastor to another and from one church to another, seeking solution to his problems. After praying with him, we agreed to pray in his village. We told him to negotiate for a motor vehicle that would take us to his village that evening so that the same car would convey us back early in the morning the next day; to enable us to be in the church on time for the next day's deliverance ministration.

The day came and we waited for him at the appointed time and place. He came very late complaining that he negotiated for a vehicle, which disappointed him and this disappointment was coming from a person who was "one of his boys" when things were fine with him. He then pleaded with us to travel by public transport. We went with him and the vehicle stopped some kilometers to our destination, as it could not go directly into the town.

Finally, God answered out prayers when one Kombi bus agreed to take us to a place near the man's house. When we were going to his personal compound, he showed us very beautiful houses built by people he had helped in his good days. When we actually got to his compound, we met an old ancestral house built by his late grandfather, which was surrounded by bush. The rooms in the house were very small with a small sitting room in the middle of the four small rooms. The whole place looked like a marine coven; so sleeping that night was not comfortable for us there.

After the prayers, he ran into some Italians and discussed with them in their language. The Italians were surprised that a Nigerian could speak their language with such fluency. They told him to go for his credentials but, according to him, all such personal documents were in Italy, which he had left ten years previously. When he left Italy for Nigeria, he had his portfolio only; and ever since then, he had been attempting to go back but he had always failed.

After discussions with him, the Italians promised to pay him about two hundred thousand naira monthly as the manger of the Nigeria branch of their company. In another state in Nigeria, this man met another oil servicing company, also from Italy, that likewise promised to employ him, with a salary of two hundred thousand naira a month. With these two offers to a man who did never have any steady job for about ten year, he became "confused" as to which to them to choose.

It appeared to him as if he was in a dream. Just one night of prayers against the evil altars in his family, doors began to open for him. He jumped out from evil altars. What you need is just a jump and you will be out. However, how long will you stay outside if sin is not dealt with (Matthew 12:43-45)? Please let no person try to jump out when he or she has not fully decided for Christ.

A woman brought a young handsome man in his twenties – a university student - to my office for counselling. The young man told me that the only breadwinner of their family came from the USA to Nigeria for a visit, but when he went back to the USA, he discovered that his well-locked bungalow was still as he had left it. Nevertheless, what highly surprised him was that he saw a sacrifice on his bed. The sacrifice included a dead rat. In addition, immediately he saw the sacrifice his health was affected. He became sick and the sickness lasted for a very long time.

His relatives in the country were going up and down to help him recover. Therefore, when the young woman came with him, I recommended deliverance prayer. After the deliverance, his brother started responding to treatment. The young man decided to visit his business partners and friend but wherever he went, people would not recognize him. Some of them even told him that they had never seen him before that day. Some forgot his name and claimed that they had never heard of a name like his.

The fact was that he was exposed to an altar when he visited Nigeria. You need to deal with all of them effectively. Some people before they were born, their parents had gone to an evil altar, knelt down before it and promised that if they got a child, he or she would automatically become theirs.

Some altars, through their priests, claim some people as their own. Some people were also dedicated to evil altars as soon as they were born. Some people's placentas were buried or dedicated to these evil altars.

A young girl once said that she was not born in Nigeria yet an evil altar was claiming her as its child. On enquiry, it was discovered that the placenta of anybody born in their village or outside it must be buried under a particular tree in that village. You have to check your background or foundation. You need to jump out to discover and fulfil your destiny.

A Nigerian woman who married a foreign professional came to me for prayers. She met the man when he arrived newly in Nigeria. After the woman had given birth to her second child and was pregnant for the third, all of a sudden, the man who abandoned his wife and four children in his country decided to go back. The woman said she pleaded with the man not to go but to no avail. As the man was moving out, the woman went to a native (occult) doctor who took her to a nearby river (in Nigeria), where with one of his legs, he opened the earth and buried something there, and assured the woman that the man would never be able to go back to his country of origin throughout his life.

Before the woman came back, the man was already waiting for her to apologize. The woman came for prayers because for fourteen years, the man had always hated to go back to his country. Moreover, as an old man without a job, the family was suffering. The woman was then of the opinion that if they all went back to the man's country, things would be better for them. After praying, she came back to tell me that the children of the man oversees who promised to send money for their travel suddenly changed their mind and became afraid; saying that what they had heard about Nigeria was fearful.

The summary of the story is that the man and members of his family (a family of seven) are still in Nigeria as at the time of writing this book. The man's destiny has been buried in Nigeria. He may even die on his way back if he insists on going back, unless he jumps out of the evil altar first.

A woman who went through our deliverance exercise some time ago gave a testimony of how her long-term incurable sickness left her. During her deliverance days, in one of her dreams, she found herself in a very big bag with one other person. She struggled for a long time before she came out. When she woke up from the dream, she became well without further medication.

It may be that you are in a grave or in a cup, well covered or buried somewhere. You need to jump out. When evil personalities lay their hands on anything belonging to you or on your fingernails, hair, etc., they can use it to deal with you on their evil altars.

# PRAYERS

1.  Anything representing me on any evil altar; jump out by fire, in the name of Jesus.

2.  Any grave altar holding my destiny; open and release me now, in the name of Jesus.

3.  I withdraw the totality of my life from any evil altar, in the name of Jesus.

4.  I take out by force all that my ancestors handed over to Satan, in the name of Jesus.

5.  Any covenant existing on any evil altar because of me; break by fire, in the name of Jesus.

6.  Blood of Jesus, repurchase me from any water altar, in the name of Jesus.

7.  By the anointing, I break every yoke tying me to any evil altar, in the name of Jesus.

8.  Resurrection power, pull me out from every evil altar, in the name of Jesus.

9.  I release fire into the chambers of the queen of the coast, in the name of Jesus.

10. My marriage, escape from any family altar, in the name of Jesus.

11.     Anything holding me on the evil altar; be roasted by fire, in the name of Jesus.

12.     Any satanic garage holding my cars; release them now, in the name of Jesus.

13.     Altars from both of my parents, tying me to bondage; be uprooted by thunder, in the name of Jesus.

14.     Satanic padlocks keeping me below my destiny; break into pieces, in the name of Jesus.

15.     My promotion, come out from the hands of my oppressors, in the name of Jesus.

16.     All my buried virtues and potentials; be exhumed by fire, in the name of Jesus.

17.     Any poison in my life from the evil altars; come out now, in the name of Jesus.

18.     You my family serpent altar; die, in the name of Jesus.

19.     Any curse following me from the evil altars; disappear now, in the name of Jesus

20.     My life, reject every evil habitation, in the name of Jesus.

21. Every curse placed upon me from evil altars; be reversed, in the name of Jesus.

22. I reject all evil manipulations from evil altars, in the name of Jesus.

23. I break and loose myself from the grip of evil altars, in the name of Jesus.

## NEW YAM FESTIVAL STORY

Twenty-one young girls, who went to sweep the communal stream, which was located in a forbidden land, were caught by the rain. In their desperation, the young girls rushed to an adjoining cave in the forbidden land to take momentary shelter. Nevertheless, the ground of the cave opened and swallowed all of them. A man who was also from the community went to the stream near the forbidden land. While he was fetching water, he saw a strange hand holding his container and trying to snatch the water container from him.

Again, there was a famous occultist from another town who entered the forbidden land and walked into the thick jungle swiftly like the hare. He got close to a large breadfruit tree. However, to his utter dismay, he saw strange faces (people) sitting on their motorcycles. They were over fifty in number, and some of them were holding what looked like a radio set in their hands.

He saw what was above his cultic powers; he jumped into a most unusual early morning conference involving unknown personalities. Suddenly, a husky, frightening voice spoke from the empting arena: "Come and take some wine." He stared at the spirit creatures, whose eyes were glittering like electric bulbs. In the midst of morbid apprehension, he mustered the last strength that was left in him and stammered in response to the mystic invitation. In addition, in less than a week after the strange encounter, the occult man lost one of his eyes and just two weeks later, the well-known occultist from a highly demonic town died.

In the same forbidden land, the breadfruit tree fell down after a torrential rain. The gigantic breadfruit tree was flat on the ground, untampered with for over six years. However, just one day, a strange noise was heard from the direction of the forbidden land. It was like thunder; like the shout of a company of soldiers preparing for war. When people visited the land the following morning, to their greatest amazement, they saw that the big breadfruit tree, which had been lying flat, was then standing completely erect.

By 1967, only two people from that village were left alive. These two men were Mark and Nwobu. It was not long after that, Mr Nwobu, of the forbidden land, died under mysterious circumstances. Mark, the only man who was still alive, called the elders of a particular church in a neighboring village and declared to them that he was not sure of surviving for a long time. He indicated that from the look of things, the goddess might take his life any moment from then. He announced to the people that any church, which had the power to take the land after his death could do so.

He was of the opinion that the land should be willed to a powerful church, which has the spiritual ability to possess it. Mark also died soon after that, leading to the extinction of all the natives of that village. The evil altars in that village were many - marine altars, forest altars, tree altars, animal altars etc. In addition, many renowned magicians, herbalists, juju doctors, charmers, necromancers, etc., from far and near could not deliver the land from the deadly altars.

Nobody, no group, or organization was courageous enough to enter the land any longer, not only because, people died mysteriously but also because it was difficult to predict the temperament of the irresistible goddess. After clearing all the lives of that village, other villages close to the land were also tautened. People became apprehensive. People began to die mysteriously in these neighboring villages.

Awesome stories of the activities of the goddess continued without interruption. As a result, nobody wanted to have anything to do with the forbidden land. On 28 June 1987, on a Saturday, a Zonal Representative of the Scripture Union, Nsukka, led his group members into the land. They entered the cave that swallowed twenty-one girls. They saw the breadfruit tree that fell down only to "rise up" again after six years.

They prayed, sang and jubilated around the land. All of them, both brothers and sisters, scattered all over the large expanse of the forbidden bush. Shouts of joy, shouts of victory and shouts of 'Hallelujah!' filled the rather silent and serene bush. Today, a mighty "signpost" is the first public indication that the land is now the bona fide property of the Scripture Union, Nigeria. You can also possess all your possessions today.

# PRAYER POINTS

# EVIL ALTARS, ENOUGH IS ENOUGH

1.  Let every satanic priest ministering against me at evil altars fall down and die, in the name of Jesus.

2.  I withdraw my name from every evil altar, in the name of Jesus.

3.  I withdraw my star from every evil altar, in the name of Jesus.

4.  Every stubborn evil altar priest; drink your own blood, in the name of Jesus.

5.  I withdraw my destiny from every evil altar, in the name of Jesus.

6.  I withdraw my blessings from every evil altar, in the name of Jesus.

7.  I withdraw my glory from every evil altar, in the name of Jesus.

I know a particular chief, who is an authority of a particular occult group in the eastern part of Nigeria. In his house, there was a particular room where only he had the right to enter. In that room, every midnight, there were voices of music. Nobody in that building dared to come out from midnight until daybreak. There used to be fearful sounds of every type of music. The chief had four sons from his first wife.

At a particular age, his first son, who was in the medical school, heard the gospel and repented. In that very year, he was supposed to be initiated into his father's occult group. While his father was battling to bring him back and hand him over to his kingdom, his second son in the same university, who was studying law, also heard the Work of God, and became a born again Christian.

The third son, an engineering student, also repented after he heard the gospel and gave his life to Christ. The last son, a pharmacy student, was also converted. The chief was left alone in his kingdom. His second wife, being a wise person, decided that his children would not live their lives under a false foundation. She took all her children and ran into a Pentecostal church.

At a stage, the occult kingdom confronted the chief and accused him of holding some powers, which he used to protect members of his family, who refused to join the occult group. The man told them that he had no other power except that his children were churchgoers.

Some of them raised an objection that their own, children also went to church. Some of such children were mad or useless; and some even died because they refused to join their father's occult group. Some of them served mass, and went to church, but they were not born again. They went to church, knew to their fingertips, all the pagan festivals, and participated in all of them. They went to church but they did not fully come to the knowledge of the Son of God, Jesus Christ.

They went to church but they were under the spell of their father's cults. They went to church, carried their bibles, but they were ignorant of the power of God in its pages.

They served God but they feared the cultic powers of their father. They were slaves to their father's idols. They went to church but the raw power in the gospel of our Lord Jesus Christ was not manifesting in them. They had wonderful Christian names but these names were only religious tags. They prayed to God but their prayers were said through Mary, the saints and other wrong routes of prayer.

They were baptized, but they were not truly born again. They believed more in their charms, the scapulars that they can see than in the Invisible God that they had not seen. They were still subject to the taboos and traditions of their father, yet they served mass every Sunday morning. They went to church but they saw nothing wrong in fornication. They still married two wives and lived a double standard lives that contradicts the Bible. Such children of occult parents run mad; some are useless, or even dead, simply because they refuse to join their father's religion or occult group.

When the occult groups argued with their leader that some powers were being hidden from them to protect their children, they were given evil powers to attack those boys. Whenever they called them in their evil altar, those boys refused to appear in their evil mirror.

During those many years of trying in vain to eliminate those boys in the evil altars, they decided to curse some aspects of their lives.

> *"And he answered and said, Must I not take heed to speak that which the LORD hath put in my mouth?" (Numbers 23:12).*

These determined, unrepentant occult evil priests began to lose a lot, having attempted to kill or destroy some aspects of the lives of these young boys in their cultic altars. Whenever they summoned them, the blood of Jesus Christ normally appeared on their behalf and burnt their cultic altars, and when they could not harm them, they demoted their father. His business began to collapse. Everything turned against him and he became angry and vowed to destroy his first son, who brought the gospel to his family.

He started dealing with the boy; manipulating his life in the evil altars. When he found out that he could not kill him, he decided to summon his MBBS exams, an exam he was going to take years ahead. He manipulated him with a desire to marry an agent of Satan and he championed it and tried to reconcile with the boy. In the process of the marriage, he reduced the boy's fire and he dealt with his destiny in the evil altars. When he programmed weakness in the boy's prayer life and his righteousness, he began to deal with his exams.

His MBBS examinations were summoned, one by one to his fifth MBBS. However, the fire of God was so much on those exam results except on his fifth MBBS exam that was to be done many years ahead. They were able to put a very little dark spot on the fifth MBBS result exam. The boy took his second MBBS to fifth MBBS and passed all his courses except surgery; a course that he was supposed to pass, having been very good at such a course.

The professor in charge of the courses happened to be a cult member. He is now the provost of that medical school and vowed never to release the result. He sat on the result of the young man and for more than twenty-five years from the day he entered the medical school, he is yet to be graduated, simply because he refused to join the Ogboni cult.

His fifth MBBS course is permanently fixed and nailed on the evil altar and unless some dangerous prayers are offered with a heart of "If I perish, I perish," that result may remain in that evil altar until the second coming of Christ. Somebody who satisfied the examiners in all the courses in the medical school except only in surgery; how come that he was victimized in surgery - a course one is not supposed to fail as a student, because it is in the process of practice that a fresh medical doctors will be perfected.

*"That made the world as a wilderness, and destroyed the cities thereof; that opened not the house of his prisoners?" (Isaiah 14:17).*

When the man finished with his first son, he faced his second son, a young brilliant lawyer, well respected in the law profession because of his truthfulness, power to marshal out facts and divine boldness. However, the young man was far much above their cultic kingdom. He slept in his law chambers to pray most of the night. His presence in the court scared away cultic lawyers, magistrates and judges. His prayer was an arrow to the cultic kingdom.

One powerful, determined occult "man decided to employ him to stand for him in court case so as to bring him close to discover his secret and to destroy him. Every effort of that man to provoke him to backslide failed. When he won a case on behalf of that cultic man, in order to provoke him to sin, the man refused to pay him what was due to him, thinking that he had to take a wrong step so that he could reduce him and kill him in the evil altar.

On one occasion, after much sacrifice, the cultic man was convinced that he must succeed, so he called the young lawyer in the evil altars and the young man appeared. When he was about to kill the lawyer, he disappeared and the man himself appeared and he stabbed himself and died. That is what we call "Back to the senders." Ever since then, the man has been trying to eliminate his own son in his evil altar but the blood of Jesus is ever ready to appear on his behalf.

If your foundation is faulty, even if you are a Christian, you need to pray aggressively to be perfectly delivered. We all have a battle to fight in order to succeed. See that big tree whose taproots go deep down into the ground, or whose branches shoot very high. Its fruitfulness and its leaves blossom for beauty. How did it grow to such a magnificent height? The light, the wind, the rain, the storm, and darkness, all had their important roles to make it what it is. We must grow amidst persecutors.

When your preaching and life expose the foolishness of occultism and their idolatry, they will persecute you. To succeed and overcome the arrows from the evil altars, we must maintain perfect holiness before God and man, in joy, peace, and faith including perseverance. With these, God will close the doors of any dungeon, and open the windows of heaven and pour down overflowing miracles, signs and wonders. Avoid distractions and live above every sin.

# THANK YOU!

I'd like to use this time to thank you for purchasing my books and helping my ministry and work. Any copy of my book you buy helps to fund my ministry and family, as well as offering much-needed inspiration to keep writing. My family and I are very thankful, and we take your assistance very seriously.

You have already accomplished so much, but I would appreciate an honest review of some of my books through the link below. This is critical since reviews reflect how much an author's work is respected.

Please [click here] to leave a review on Amazon. If you're viewing from a printed version, please visit amazon.com/review/create-review?asin=1650596138 to leave a review.

Please be aware that I read and value all comments and reviews. You can always post a review even though you haven't finished the book yet, and then edit your reviews later.

Thank you so much as you spare a precious moment of your time and may God bless you and meet you at the very point of your need.

You can also send me an email to hello@madueke.com if you encounter any difficulty while writing your review.

# PRAYER M. MADUEKE'S BESTSELLING BOOKS

Click on any of the [Buy Now] buttons to view or purchase them on my website. If you're viewing from a printed version, please visit madueke.com and search for these books.

1. Dictionary of Demons & Complete Deliverance — [Buy Now]

2. Monitoring Spirits — [Buy Now]

3. Praying with The Blood of Jesus — [Buy Now]

4. The Power of Speaking in Tongues — [Buy Now]

5. Speaking Things into Existence by Faith — [Buy Now]

6. Discerning and Defeating the Ahab & Jezebel Spirit — [Buy Now]

7. Defeating the Python Spirit — [Buy Now]

8. 35 Special Dangerous Decrees — [Buy Now]

9. 21/40 Nights of Decrees and Your Enemies Will Surrender — [Buy Now]

10. Command the Morning, Day and Night    [Buy Now]

11. Evil Summon    [Buy Now]

12. Overcoming & Destroying the Spirit of Rejection & Hatred    [Buy Now]

13. Queen of Heaven: Wife of Satan    [Buy Now]

14. The False Prophet    [Buy Now]

15. Dominion Over Sickness & Disease    [Buy Now]

16. The Battle Plan for Destroying Foundational Witchcraft    [Buy Now]

17. The Queen of the Coast    [Buy Now]

18. Dictionary of Unmerited Favor    [Buy Now]

19. Prayers for Breakthrough in your Business    [Buy Now]

20. A Jump From Evil Altar    [Buy Now]

21. 100 Days Prayers to Wake Up Your Lazarus    [Buy Now]

22. Breaking Evil Yokes    [Buy Now]

37. Prayers for Good Health                          [Buy Now]

38. Comprehensive Deliverance                        [Buy Now]

39. Prayers for College and University
    Students                                         [Buy Now]

40. 40 Prayer Giants                                 [Buy Now]

41. Divine Protection & Immunity While
    Sleeping                                         [Buy Now]

42. Prayers for Fertility in your Marriage           [Buy Now]

43. More Kingdoms to Conquer                         [Buy Now]

44. Confront and Conquer your Enemy                  [Buy Now]

45. Prayers to Raise Godly Children                  [Buy Now]

# 4 Free Ebooks

In order to say a 'Thank You' for purchasing *A Jump from Evil Altar*, I offer these books to you in appreciation. Click or type madueke.com/free-gift in your browser.

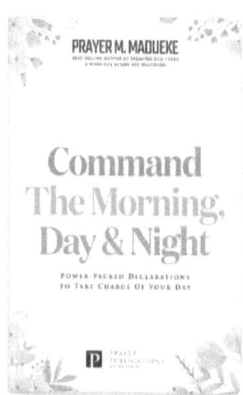

# Video Access Bonus

As promised, I have prepared exclusive video content to complement the topics covered in the book you purchased. These videos offer deeper insights and discussions to enhance your learning experience.

To access your free course on *"Breaking Free from Evil Altars,"* please follow these steps:

1. Click or type the following link into your browser: **madueke.com/courses/breaking-free-from-evil-altars**

2. You will be directed to the course page on my website.

3. Add the course to your cart by clicking on the **"ACCESS COURSE NOW"** button and you'll be directed to the checkout page automatically.

4. On the checkout page, apply the coupon code **"bfevilaltc100off"** to get the course for free.

5. Complete the checkout process, and you will gain instant access to the course videos.

If you encounter any difficulties or have any questions, please feel free to reach out to me here: hello@madueke.com. I'm here to assist you every step of the way.

# Message from the Author

I want to see you succeed, grow, and break free from negativity and obstacles. My hope is for you to thrive, unaffected by negative influences and challenging situations. Because of that, please permit me to introduce two courses that I believe passionately will help you:

1.  To break the evil altars and powers of your father's house, The role of altars in the realm of existence is very key because altars are meeting places between the physical and the spiritual, between the visible and the invisible.

    Unless a man cuts off the evil flow from the power of his father's house, he will not fulfil his destiny. Click here to learn more about my course on how to tear down unholy altars and close the enemy's entryways into your life!

2.  To help you seamlessly break iron-like problems, illness, delayed marriage, poverty, or any long-standing battle.

    Discover the transformative power of Christian fasting and prayer. Remember, Matthew 17:21 teaches us, *"But this kind of demon does not go out except by prayer and fasting."* Ready to overcome your struggles? <u>Click here</u> to learn more about this course.

Embrace the journey ahead with faith, for through prayer, fasting, and the dismantling of evil altars, you shall unlock the doors to spiritual liberation and divine breakthrough. May your path be illuminated by His grace as you walk towards a life free from bondage.

If you're seeing this from the physical copy, type the link: <u>madueke.com/courses</u> in your browser to view all the courses on my website.

**Prayer Madueke**
CHRISTIAN AUTHOR

# Christian Counselling

We were created for a greater purpose than only survival and God wants us to live a full life.

If you need prayer or counselling, or if you have any other inquiries, please visit the counselling page on my website to know when I will be available for a phone call.

Click or type links.madueke.com/counselling in your browser.

# Let's Connect on Youtube ▶

Join me on my YouTube channel, "Prayer M. Madueke," where I share powerful insights, guidance, and prayers for spiritual breakthroughs.

Subscribe today to unlock the secrets of the Kingdom and embrace an abundant life. Let's grow together!

Click or type links.madueke.com/youtube in your browser.

# An Invitation to Become a Ministry Partner

I appreciate the support and inquiries I have received regarding collaboration with my ministry. Your prayers and dedication to the work of the Kingdom are highly valued.

You can also visit the donation page on my website if you would like to contribute or learn more about supporting my ministry: madueke.com/donate.

Thank you for your continued support and faithfulness in Christ Jesus.

www.ingramcontent.com/pod-product-compliance
Lightning Source LLC
Chambersburg PA
CBHW021616120626
46545CB00001B/250

* 9 7 8 1 9 6 4 5 8 4 1 0 2 *